AN

ELEMENTARY TREATISE

ON

MECHANICS.

BY I. W. JACKSON,
PROFESSOR OF MATHEMATICS IN UNION COLLEGE.

ALBANY:
PUBLISHED BY GRAY, SPRAGUE & CO.

1852.

RIGGS, PRINTER, SCHENECTADY.

ADVERTISEMENT.

THE following exposition of the elementary principles of rational mechanics, is intended to be sufficiently brief and free from difficulties to be thoroughly mastered by students of ordinary capacity, in the time usually allotted to the subject, and yet comprehensive enough to be made the basis of a course of general physics and practical mechanics. It has no claims to originality; the methods employed being generally those which have been long in use, and which may be found in many of the best treatises on the same subject.

Of the works consulted in the preparation of this volume, most assistance has been derived from those of POISSON and BOUCHARLAT: occasional use has also been made of those of EARNSHAW, POTTER, SAURI, and PUISSANT.

In the present emission, the subject of solids only is considered. The few sections on fluids, necessary to complete the plan, will soon be published.

TABLE OF CONTENTS.

INTRODUCTION.

PART FIRST.

STATICS.

PART SECOND.

DYNAMICS.

ELEMENTS OF MECHANICS.

INTRODUCTION.

1. WHEN a body occupies successively different positions in space, it is said to be in motion.

2. Whatever produces, or tends to produce motion, is called *force.* The action of a force, whatever its origin, may be conceived to consist in communicating to the body on which it acts, impulses, either finite, or infinitely small. The body is, in all cases, supposed to be entirely inert, and subject only to the influence of forces exterior to itself.*

3. It can readily be conceived that two or more forces may be so applied to a body, that their effects shall counteract each other, and no motion shall ensue: in this case the forces are said to be in *equilibrium.*

4. Mechanics is the science which treats of equilibrium and of motion. It is divided into two parts, STATICS and DYNAMICS.

*Abstraction is thus made of vitality, and certain properties inherent in matter, as gravity, and the chemical and electrical attractions, etc. etc. When the effects of these are to be determined, they are regarded as extraneous forces.

5. In statics, the subject of equilibrium is considered. It is divided into two parts:

I. The statics of solids, called simply *Statics;*

II. The statics of fluids, called *Hydrostatics.*

6. In dynamics, the subject of motion is considered. It also is divided into two parts:

I. The dynamics of solids, called simply *Dynamics;*

II. The dynamics of fluids, or *Hydrodynamics.*

7. The reasonings in mechanics are based upon certain facts of great generality, derived from observation and experiment, called *the laws of motion.* We shall do little more than enunciate them, leaving it chiefly to the instructor to supply the observations and experiments by which they are proved and illustrated.

LAWS OF MOTION.

I. *The law of inertia.*

The motion of a body, when left to itself, is rectilinear and uniform. Thus when a body receives an impulse and then is abandoned to itself, according to this law all its points will describe straight lines, and will move over equal spaces in equal times.

At first view, this law appears to be contrary to the most obvious facts; for the motions which we observe in bodies on the surface of the earth are neither rectilinear nor uniform, and they all soon terminate. In these cases, however, the bodies are really not left to themselves, but are constantly acted upon by certain forces, as gravity, friction, etc., which in a greater or less degree interfere with their motions. But it is invariably found, that as these interfering forces are diminished in intensity, the motions take place more nearly in accordance with the law. Thus in the case of a body moving on a horizontal plane, as the surface of each is rendered smoother, the more nearly does the motion become rectilinear, and the longer does it continue. Again, a pendulum, oscillating under ordinary circumstances, is soon brought to rest; but if we diminish the friction at the axis of suspension, and cause the vibrations to be made in the vacuum of an air-pump, the motion will continue for many hours.

From these and other similar experiments, as well as from numerous analogous observations, we infer that if the interfering forces could be annihilated, the motions would take place in conformity with the law.

II. *The law of the coexistence or independence of motions.* The relative motions of a system of bodies are not affected by any motion which is common to all the points of the system.

To aid the student in the conception of this law, suppose a number of bodies to be in motion on a surface, plane or curved, and conceive the surface to be at the same time moving parallel to itself; then, according to this law, the motions of the bodies on the surface, or their relative motions, will not be affected by the motion which they have in common with the surface, but will take place in the same manner as if the surface were at rest. The surface having been introduced merely to render the distinction between the relative motions of the bodies and their common motion more obvious, it may now be withdrawn, if in its place we give to each of the bodies a motion identical with the common motion. We shall thus have a system of bodies moving in space in the manner supposed in the enunciation.

A case less general than the preceding, but one to which it will be necessary frequently to refer, is that in which we suppose a point to be moving on a straight line, and the line to be carried at the same time with a uniform rectilinear motion parallel to itself; the motion of the point, according to this law, taking place as it would were the line at rest.

An apt illustration of this law is furnished by a vessel sailing in a given direction, in which the motions of bodies relative to the parts of the vessel take place in precisely the same manner as if the vessel were at rest, though, in addition to their relative motions, the bodies all have the same motion as the vessel. Since the vessel may obviously be regarded merely as the means of communicating motion to the bodies, we may suppose it to be withdrawn, if at the same time we suppose the bodies to retain their common motion.

III. *The law of the equality of action and reaction.*

To every action, there is always opposed an equal reaction.

According to this law, when a body rests upon an immovable plane, the pressure of the body upon the plane causes in the plane a re-action, in virtue of which the plane may be said to press upwards with the same force that the body presses downwards. In like manner, when a body falls upon an immovable plane, the plane reacts with a force equal and opposite to that with which it is struck by the body.

Also when two bodies, moving in the same line, come in collision, the effects upon the bodies, *properly estimated*,* are equal, and take place in opposite directions.

*The method of estimating the effects will be explained in a subsequent article.

PART FIRST.

STATICS.

---

8. By the term *material point*, or *particle*, is meant the smallest conceivable portion of matter. In mechanics, any one material point is conceived to be exactly similar to every other material point. A body may be regarded as a collection of material points.

In considering the effects of forces, we first suppose the forces applied to a single material point. This point we regard as entirely passive, and subject only to the action of the forces under consideration.

In a force, three things are to be considered: its *point of application*, its *direction*, and its *intensity*.

The point of application of a force is the material point on which it acts.

The direction of a force is the direction in which it tends to move its point of application.

The intensity of a force is its capacity of producing motion.

Two forces are regarded as equal in intensity, when, acting separately upon two material points, they cause the points to describe equal spaces in equal times.

Two equal forces applied to the same point, and acting in the same direction, constitute a double force; three equal forces, a triple force; four a quadruple force, and so on. Taking one of the equal forces for the unit of intensity, and representing it by 1 or by p, the intensities of the double, triple, quadruple, etc. forces, will be represented by 2, 3, 4, etc., or $2p$, $3p$, $4p$, etc. The intensities of forces may thus be represented by numbers or algebraic symbols, and may be made the subject of arithmetical and algebraic operations.

The intensities of forces may also be represented by straight lines; a given straight line being assumed to represent the unit of intensity, and a double, triple, quadruple, etc. force being represented by a line of double, triple, quadruple, etc. the length of the assumed line.

According to the second law of motion, double, triple, quadruple, etc. forces cause the material points to which they are applied to describe, in a given time, spaces double, triple, quadruple, etc. the space due to the unit of intensity. The spaces described by the material points are thus directly proportional to the intensities of the forces; and consequently the same lines which represent the intensities of the forces may also be employed to represent the spaces described by the material points to which the forces are applied.

If, for example, the lines AB, AC, AD [Fig. 1], represent the intensities P, Q and R of three forces referred to a common unit, they may also be employed to represent the spaces which these forces severally would cause a material point to describe in a given time.

The converse also is obviously true, viz. that if AB, AC and AD represent the spaces which three forces, whose intensities are P, Q and R, cause a material point to describe in a given time, the same lines may also be employed to represent the intensities P, Q and R respectively.

9. Conceive now a material point to be moving uniformly on the straight line A′B′ [Fig. 1], and suppose the line to be at the same time moving parallel to itself with a uniform rectilinear motion; then by the second law of motion, the motion of the point on the line will be entirely unaffected by the motion which it has in common with the line; and hence if we represent the motions of the point and line during any time t by AB and AC respectively, at the end of that time the point will evidently be at D, having described the diagonal AD of the parallelogram constructed on AB and AC. But if we abstract the line A′B′, and the motion which the point has in common with it, and suppose the point to be moving alone in space in the direction A′B′, at the same rate as before, and to receive when it arrives at A an impulse, such as would cause it, were it at rest, to describe the line AC in the time t, the final result will

evidently be unaffected; and in virtue of the two motions, the point, at the end of the time *t*, will still be found at D. Again, if, instead of supposing the point to be in motion when it receives the impulse in the direction AC, we suppose it to be at rest at A, and to receive at the same instant another impulse, such, as acting alone, would cause it to describe in the time *t* the line AB, it is still obvious that in virtue of the two impulses the point will, as before, describe with a uniform motion the diagonal of the parallelogram ABDC, and at the end of the time *t* be found at D.

Let now the intensities of the forces to which the motions AB and AC are due, be represented by *P* and *Q*; and as the motion from A to D may also be attributed to a single force, let the intensity of that force be denoted by *R*: then the forces *P*, *Q* and *R** may be represented by the lines AB, AC and AD; and instead of saying the forces *P*, *Q* and *R*, we may say the forces AB, AC and AD. *R*, or AD, is called *the resultant* of *P* and *Q*, or of AB and AC; and *P* and *Q*, or AB and AC, are called *the components* of *R*, or AD. The characteristic property of the resultant is that it may be substituted for the components. Thus the effect upon the point A is precisely the same whether the components *P* and *Q* act upon it in the directions AB and AC, or the resultant *R* acts upon it in the direction AD.

*Hereafter, for the sake of brevity, we shall say simply the force *P*, the force *Q*, etc., instead of the force whose intensity is *P*, *Q*, etc.

The result at which we have arrived, may now be thus enunciated :

The resultant of two forces applied to a material point, and represented by lines measured from this point on their directions, is represented in magnitude and direction by the diagonal of the parallelogram constructed on these lines.

This proposition is called the *parallelogram of forces.*

The forces P and Q may evidently be supposed to be either finite, or infinitely small.

If A be a fixed point, P and Q will exert upon it a pressure of longer or shorter duration, the measure of which is evidently R.*

10. In figure 2, in which AI is taken equal to AB or P, as the angle BAC diminishes, ID tends constantly to become equal to BD or Q, and hence R to become equal to $P + Q$.

In figure 3, in which AI is taken equal to AD or R, as the angle BAC increases to 180°, BI tends constantly to become equal to BD or Q, and R to become equal to $P - Q$.

Hence, when the forces P and Q act in the same straight line, it may be inferred from the above proposition that the resultant is equal to their sum or difference, according as they act in the same or opposite directions. This result may also be deduced immediately from the second law of motion.

*When P and Q are forces of the kind commonly called *impulsive*, such, for example, as that exerted in driving a nail with a hammer, the duration of the pressure is very brief, though finite : when they are of the same nature as gravity, the pressure is continuous.

When the forces act in opposite directions, we have

$$R = P - Q.$$

But P may be considered as the resultant of two forces P' and p, both acting in the same direction as P; and p as the resultant of two others P'' and p', both acting in the same direction as p, and so on. The same is also true of Q; hence we have

$$R = P' + P'' + P''' + \text{etc.} - Q' - Q'' - Q''' - \text{etc.} \ldots\ldots [1]$$

When the forces P', P'', etc., Q', Q'', etc., are in equilibrium, we have $R = 0$; and hence

$$P' + P'' + P''' + \text{etc.} = Q' + Q'' + Q''' + \text{etc.}$$

is the equation which expresses the condition of equilibrium of any number of forces which act in the same straight line.

11. Resuming the consideration of the parallelogram of forces: Since [Fig. 4] BD is equal to AC, we have the three forces P, Q and R represented by the sides of the triangle ABD. Moreover we perceive that the angle at B is the supplement of the angle BAC formed by the directions of the components P and Q, and that the angle ADB is equal to the angle DAC which the direction of Q makes with that of R. Hence of the three forces P, Q and R, and the angles comprehended between their directions, any three being given, one of the three at least being a force, the remaining three can be determined by solving the triangle ABD.

Thus denoting the angles which the directions of P and Q make with the direction of R, by b and c, and the angle which they make with each other by a; if P, Q and a are given, and R and b are required, to determine the latter, we have

$$R^2 = P^2 + Q^2 - 2PQ \cdot \cos B$$
$$= P^2 + Q^2 + 2PQ \cdot \cos a,$$

and $$R : Q :: \sin a : \sin b.$$

12. When three forces P, Q and R' [Fig. 4], are in equilibrium about a point A, any one of them, as R', must evidently be equal and directly opposite to the resultant of the other two. But employing the same notation as in the preceding articles, and denoting the supplements of b and c by b' and c', we have

$$R : P :: \sin a : \sin c$$
$$:: \sin a : \sin c',$$

and $$R : Q :: \sin a : \sin b$$
$$:: \sin a : \sin b';$$

and hence, since $R = R'$,

$$R' : P : Q :: \sin a : \sin c' : \sin b'.$$

That is, *when three forces are in equilibrium about the same point, each of them may be represented by the sine of the angle comprehended between the directions of the other two.*

13. Any number of given forces P, P', P'', P''', etc., applied at a point, and situated in the same or in different planes, may, by means of the parallelogram of forces, be reduced to a single force. We first determine the resultant R of any two of them, as P and

P'; then the resultant R', of R and any one of the remaining forces, as P''; and so on till all the given forces have been compounded: the last resultant will be the resultant of the system.

Figure 5 presents a case in which four forces P, P', P'', P''', are reduced to a single force R''. An inspection of the figure shows that the resultant may be determined by the following construction: The lines AB, AB′, AB″, AB‴, representing the four forces: through the point B, draw BC equal and parallel to AB′; through C, draw CD equal and parallel to AB″; and through D draw DE equal and parallel to AB‴: the straight line joining the points E and A is the resultant required. This method of finding the resultant is applicable to any number of forces.

We have just seen that any number of forces applied at a point may be reduced to a single force, or *resultant*. The converse also is evidently true, viz. that a single force applied at a point may be resolved into any number of forces, or *components*, all acting upon the same point, and producing the same effect as the single force.

---

14. METHODS OF DETERMINING THE POSITION OF A POINT.

A convenient and elegant method of treating the subject of forces, consists in decomposing the forces into separate systems, parallel to certain assumed straight lines. The application of this method requires a knowledge of the first principles of analytic geometry, of which we shall here give a brief exposition.

§ 1. *Method of determining the position of a point on a line.*

The position of a point on a given straight line XX′ [Fig. 6], is evidently determined when we know its distance from an assumed point O of the line, and the direction in which the distance is to be laid off from the assumed point. The method of indicating the direction is conventional, and consists in affecting the distance with the sign plus or minus, according as the point is situated to the right or left of O. Thus, employing the letter x, as the general symbol denoting the distance, the equation

$$x = + a$$

determines a point M, situated to the right of O, at a distance from it equal to a linear units; and the equation

$$x = - a$$

determines a point M′, situated at the same distance from O, in the opposite direction.

§ 2. *Method of determining the position of a point on a plane.*

The position of a point on a plane is determined when we know its distances, affected with their proper signs, from two straight lines drawn in the plane at right angles to each other.

Let XX′, YY′ [Fig. 7] represent these lines, forming by their intersection the four right angles XOY,

YOX′, X′OY′, Y′OX. Consider the point M situated in the angle XOY, and draw through it the straight lines MP, MQ, parallel respectively to the lines YY′, XX′, and intersecting them in the points P and Q. Then it is evident that when P and Q are given, the point M can be determined by drawing through them the straight lines MP, MQ, parallel to YY′, XX′ respectively; it being at the intersection of these lines. But P and Q are given when the distances OP and OQ, or MQ and MP, are given: thus the point M is determined by its distances from the lines XX′, YY′.

The line OP or MQ is called *the abscissa,* and OQ or MP *the ordinate,* of the point M. The abscissa and ordinate, taken together, are called *the co-ordinates* of M. The line XX′ is called *the axis of abscissas,* and YY′ *the axis of ordinates,* and together they are called *the axes of co-ordinates.* The point O in which the axes intersect, is called *the origin of co-ordinates.* The general symbols, commonly employed to denote the abscissas and ordinates, are x and y; and hence the axis XX′ is frequently called the axis of x, and YY′ the axis of y. The axis XX′ is usually supposed to be horizontal.

The quantities x and y are supposed to be capable of assuming all possible values, both positive and negative; and according to the method of the preceding section [§ 1], the positive values of x are laid off on XX′ from O to the right, the negative values from O to the left; the positive values of y are laid off on YY′ from O upwards, the negative values from O downwards. Thus, denoting the values of x and y, in any particular case, by a and b,

when $x = + a$ and $y = + b$, the point is in the 1st angle;
" $x = - a$ and $y = + b$, " " 2d " ;
" $x = - a$ and $y = - b$, " " 3d " ;
" $x = + a$ and $y = - b$, " " 4th " .
When $x = + a$ and $y = 0$, the point is on the axis of x;
" $x = 0$ and $y = + b$, " " " y;
" $x = 0$ and $y = 0$, the point is at the origin.

§ 3. *Method of determining the position of a point in space.*

The position of a point in space is determined when we know its distances, affected with their proper signs, from three planes drawn through an assumed point at right angles to each other.

Let XOY, XOZ, YOZ [Fig. 8] be the three fixed planes intersecting each other, when sufficiently produced, in the lines XX′, YY′, ZZ′, and determining by their intersection eight trihedral angles. Consider the point M situated in the angle O – XYZ, and draw through it three planes parallel to the fixed planes, viz:

MM′QM‴ parallel to the plane XOZ, and cutting the line YY′ in Q;
MM′PM″ parallel to the plane YOZ, and cutting the line XX′ in P;
and MM″RM‴ parallel to the plane XOY, and cutting the line ZZ′ in R.

Then it is evident that the point M can be determined, when the points Q, P and R are known; for, drawing through these points three planes parallel respectively to the fixed planes, they will intersect each other at the point M. But the points P, Q and R are known when the distances OP, OQ and OR, or the equal lines MM‴, MM″, MM′, are given: thus the point M is determined in position by its distances from the three fixed planes.

The distances OP, OQ and OR are called *the co-ordinates* of the point M; the lines XX′, YY′, ZZ′, are called *the axes of co-ordinates;* and the planes XOY, XOZ, YOZ, are called *the co-ordinate planes.* The point O is called *the origin.* The co-ordinates OP, OQ and OR are denoted by the general symbols x, y and z respectively; and hence the fixed planes are denominated the planes of xy, xz and yz respectively. The plane of xy is generally supposed to be horizontal. The positive values of x, y and z are laid off, according to the conventional method, on the several axes from O towards the points X, Y and Z respectively, and the negative values from O in the opposite directions.

The signs of the co-ordinates of a point determine in which of the eight angles the point is situated. Thus, denoting the numerical values of x, y and z, in a particular case, by a, b and c:

when $x = a$, $y = b$, and $z = c$, the point is situated in the angle O - XYZ;

when $x = -a$, $y = -b$, and $z = -c$, it is situated in the angle O - X′Y′Z′.

When one of the co-ordinates is zero, the point is situated in the plane of the other two co-ordinates;

thus when $x = a$, $y = b$, and $z = 0$, the point is in the plane of xy. When two of the co-ordinates are each equal to zero, the point is on the axis of the third co-ordinate; thus when $x = a$, $y = 0$, and $z = 0$, it is on the axis of x. When $x = 0$, $y = 0$, and $z = 0$, the point is at the origin.

OF FORCES SITUATED IN THE SAME PLANE, AND APPLIED AT THE SAME POINT.

15. Let O [Fig. 9] be the point of application of the forces; and through it, in the plane of the forces, let the co-ordinate axes XX′, YY′ be drawn.

The direction of a force P is determined by the angles which it makes with OX and OY, the parts of the axes on which the positive co-ordinates are laid off, the angles being reckoned on both sides of these lines from 0 to 180°. Thus, considering the four distinct cases which can occur, as represented in figures 9, 10, 11, 12:

When the direction of the force is situated in the angle XOY, its position is determined by the angles XOM, YOM;

when in the angle YOX′, it is determined by the angles XOM′, YOM′;

when in the angle X′OY′, it is determined by the angles XOM″, YOM″;

when in the angle XOY′, it is determined by the angles XOM‴, YOM‴.

Let now the force P, in the several cases, be represented by the equal lines OM, OM′, OM″, OM‴; and let it be decomposed into the components OB or OB′, OC or OC′, coincident respectively with the two axes. Then we perceive that the components coincident with XX′ act, when the force is situated in the 1st or 4th angle, from O to the right; when in the 2d or 3d angle, from O to the left: also that the components coincident with YY′ act, when the force is situated in the 1st or 2d angle, from O upwards; when in the 3d or 4th, from O downwards.

When, therefore, two or more forces, acting upon the point O, are decomposed in directions coincident with the axes, there may be two sets of components in the direction of each axis, the components of one set acting in one direction, those of the other in the direction opposite. Considering the components which act in the line XX′: if we affect those acting in opposite directions with opposite signs, as, for example, those which act from O to the right, with the sign plus +, and those which act from O to the left with the sign minus −; then the resultant will evidently be equal to the algebraic sum of the components. The same is true of the components which act in the line YY′.

But the values of the components determined by the usual method, will necessarily be affected with the proper signs. Thus, denoting generally the angles which the direction of P makes with OX and OY by α and β, when the force is situated in the first angle, we have

$$\text{OB} = P \cos \text{BOM} = + P \cos \alpha,$$
$$\text{OC} = P \cos \text{COM} = + P \cos \beta;$$

when it is situated in the second angle, we have

$$OB' = P\cos B'OM' = -P\cos\alpha,$$
$$OC = P\cos COM' = +P\cos\beta;$$

when in the third, we have

$$OB' = P\cos B'OM'' = -P\cos\alpha,$$
$$OC' = P\cos C'OM'' = -P\cos\beta;$$

when in the fourth,

$$OB = P\cos BOM''' = +P\cos\alpha,$$
$$OC' = P\cos C'OM''' = -P\cos\beta.$$

Now let there be any number of forces P, P', P'', etc. [Fig. 13], acting upon the point O, in the directions OM, OM', OM'', etc.; and let the angles which their directions make with the axes be denoted by α, α', α'', etc., β, β', β'', etc.; then if we denote the algebraic sum of the components which act in XX' by X, and that of the components which act in YY' by Y, we shall have

$$X = P\cos\alpha + P'\cos\alpha' + P''\cos\alpha'' + \text{etc.}, \ldots\ldots\ [3]$$
$$Y = P\cos\beta + P'\cos\beta' + P''\cos\beta'' + \text{etc.} \ \ldots\ldots\ [4]$$

These equations are general. In a given case, the values of the angles will determine the algebraic signs of the terms of the second members. A common method of denoting the algebraic sum of a series of terms, all of which are of the same form, is to write only a single term preceded by the Greek letter Σ. Applying this method to the above equation, we have

$$X = \Sigma\ (P\cos\alpha),$$
$$Y = \Sigma\ (P\cos\beta).$$

We have now reduced the forces P, P', P'', etc. to the two forces X and Y, acting at right angles to each other; and if we represent X by OE [Fig. 13], and Y by OF, the resultant R of these two forces will be represented by the diagonal OG of the rectangle OEGF. This resultant will be the resultant of the system P, P', P'', etc., and will be determined in intensity by the equation

$$R = \sqrt{X^2 + Y^2}. \quad \ldots\ldots\ldots\ldots\ldots\ldots \quad [5]$$

To find the angles a and b which the direction of R makes with the axes, we have

$$\cos a = \frac{X}{R}, \quad \cos b = \frac{Y}{R}. \quad \ldots\ldots\ldots\ldots\ldots \quad [6]$$

The quantities R, a and b, are thus completely determined.

16. *Conditions of equilibrium.*

In order that P, P', P'', etc. may be in equilibrium about the point O, their resultant must evidently be equal to zero; a condition which gives

$$X^2 + Y^2 = 0.$$

But as the square of a quantity is essentially positive, this equation can be satisfied only by making X and Y separately equal to zero; thus the conditions of equilibrium are expressed by the equations

$$X = 0, \quad Y = 0.$$

Of forces applied at the same point, and situated in different planes.

17. Let the three forces X, Y, Z, be applied at the point O [Fig. 14], and be represented in intensity and direction by the lines OS, OS′, OS″. On these lines as adjacent edges, construct the parallelopiped RS. Then it is evident that ON the diagonal of the base OSNS′ is the resultant of OS and OS′, that is, of X and Y; and that ON′ the diagonal of the parallelopiped is the resultant of ON and OS″, that is, of X, Y and Z. Thus the resultant of the forces X, Y and Z, represented by the lines OS, OS′, and OS″, is the diagonal of the parallelopiped constructed on these lines. If the directions of the three forces intersect each other at right angles, the parallelopiped will be rectangular; and denoting the resultant ON′ by R, we shall have

$$R = \sqrt{X^2 + Y^2 + Z^2}.$$

The direction of a force P situated in space, and applied at the point O [Fig. 15], is determined by the angles which it makes with the lines OX, OY, OZ, the parts of the co-ordinate axes drawn through O, on which the positive co-ordinates are laid off, the angles being reckoned from 0 to 180°. Thus if P is situated in the angle O – XYZ, its direction OM is determined by the angles XOM, YOM, ZOM, each angle being less than 90°; if it is situated in the angle O – XYZ′, its direction OM, is determined by the angles $XOM_{\prime\prime}$, $YOM_{\prime\prime}$, $Z'OM_{\prime\prime}$, the first two being each less than 90°, the third greater than 90°.*

If the intensity of P be represented by OM, its three rectangular components in the directions of the axes will evidently be OP, OQ and OR; and if the angles which it makes with the axes be denoted by α, β and γ respectively, we shall have

$$OP = OM \, . \cos MOP = P \cos \alpha,$$

$$OQ = OM \, . \cos MOQ = P \cos \beta,$$

$$OR = OM \, . \cos MOR = P \cos \gamma.$$

Now let the forces P, P', P'', etc. be applied at the point O, and let the angles which their directions make with the co-ordinate axes be denoted by α, β, γ; α', β', γ'; α'', β'', γ'', etc.: then the components coincident with XX′ will be

$$P \cos \alpha, \quad P' \cos \alpha', \quad P'' \cos \alpha'', \text{ etc.};$$

those coincident with YY′ will be

$$P \cos \beta, \quad P' \cos \beta', \quad P'' \cos \beta'', \text{ etc.};$$

and those coincident with ZZ′ will be

$$P \cos \gamma, \quad P' \cos \gamma', \quad P'' \cos \gamma'', \text{ etc.};$$

and if the algebraic sums of the components in the several directions be denoted by X, Y and Z respectively, we shall have

*The angles which the direction of P makes with the axes OX, OY, fix its position on two conic surfaces, of which O is the common vertex; and OX and OY the axes: these surfaces intersect each other in two straight lines, and the third angle determines which of the two lines is the direction sought. Thus a certain relation exists between the three angles. In accordance with our plan, this, like many other parts of the general subject, is left to be developed either by the pupil or his instructor.

$$\left.\begin{aligned} X &= P\cos\alpha + P'\cos\alpha' + P''\cos\alpha'' + \text{etc.} = \Sigma\,(P\cos\alpha), \\ Y &= P\cos\beta + P'\cos\beta' + P''\cos\beta'' + \text{etc.} = \Sigma\,(P\cos\beta), \\ Z &= P\cos\gamma + P'\cos\gamma' + P''\cos\gamma'' + \text{etc.} = \Sigma\,(P\cos\gamma), \end{aligned}\right\}\;..[7]$$

If we denote by R the resultant of X, Y, Z, that is, of P, P', P'', etc., we shall have

$$R = \sqrt{X^2 + Y^2 + Z^2};$$

and if we denote the angles which the direction of R makes with the three axes by a, b and c respectively, we shall have

$$\cos a = \frac{X}{R}, \quad \cos b = \frac{Y}{R}, \quad \cos c = \frac{Z}{R}, \;\ldots\ldots\ldots\ldots [8]$$

and thus the resultant will be completely determined.*

18. *Conditions of equilibrium.*

In order that the forces may be in equilibrium, R must be equal to zero; a condition which gives

$$X^2 + Y^2 + Z^2 = 0,$$

and hence $\quad X = 0, \;\; Y = 0, \;\; Z = 0.$

If the point O is not entirely free, but subject to the condition of remaining on a given surface, it is not essential to an equilibrium that the resultant should be equal to zero: it is only necessary that it should act towards the surface, and at right angles to it. The resistance of the surface is equal and directly opposite to R.

19. As yet we have constantly supposed the forces

*The understanding of this article may be greatly facilitated by a model of the co-ordinate planes, which the student himself can easily construct of pieces of pasteboard.

under consideration to be applied at the same point. We shall now suppose them applied at different points; the points being conceived to be so connected, that their positions with respect to each other are invariable. The lines of direction of the forces may be parallel to each other, or oblique. We shall first consider the case in which they are parallel.

OF PARALLEL FORCES.

20. Let P and Q be any two parallel forces, applied at the extremities A and B [Fig. 16] of an inflexible straight line AB, and acting in the same sense* in the lines AV and BS, and let their intensities be represented by the lines AU and BT.

Without affecting the action of these forces, we may apply at A and B in AB produced, two equal and opposite forces AM and BN. The resultants AD and BI of the four forces AM, AU, BN, BT, may then be transferred along their lines of direction (produced backwards) to C their point of meeting, and there be resolved into the four forces CG, CL, CH, CK, equal and parallel respectively to the four forces applied at A and B; but CH and CG being

*When the lines of direction of forces are parallel, we use the word *sense* to indicate the relations of the directions: thus when two parallel forces act towards the same parts of space, both to the right or both to the left, for example, we say they act *in the same sense;* when they act towards opposite parts of space, we say they act *in opposite senses.* When we speak of the directions of parallel forces, we mean their lines of direction.

equal, and acting in the same line and in opposite directions, destroy each other: hence the resultant of the system is CL + CK, or $P + Q$, acting in the same sense as the given forces, and in the line CO parallel to their lines of direction.

The resultant may evidently be supposed to be applied at O, where its direction intersects the line AB. To determine this point, we have from the similar triangles AUD, COA, BTI, COB,

$$\text{AU} : \text{UD} :: \text{CO} : \text{OA},$$

$$\text{BT} : \text{TI} :: \text{CO} : \text{OB};$$

or

$$\text{UD} \times \text{CO} = \text{AU} \times \text{OA},$$

$$\text{TI} \times \text{CO} = \text{BT} \times \text{OB};$$

and hence

$$P \times \text{OA} = Q \times \text{OB},$$

or

$$P : Q :: \text{OB} : \text{OA}.$$

That is, O, *the point of application of the resultant, divides the line* AB *into parts reciprocally proportional to the intensities of the component forces.*

The above proportion, it will be perceived, is independent of the angle which the directions of the forces make with AB, and is true for any straight line drawn through O and terminated by their directions.

Resuming the proportion,

$$P : Q :: \text{OB} : \text{OA},$$

we get by composition,

$$P : P + Q :: \text{OB} : \text{OB} + \text{OA},$$

or, denoting $P + Q$ by R,

$$P : R :: \text{OB} : \text{AB}.$$

In like manner we get

$$Q : R :: \text{OA} : \text{AB};$$

and hence we have

$$P : Q : R :: \text{OB} : \text{OA} : \text{AB}.$$

If the force P be represented by OB, the forces Q and R will be represented by OA and AB respectively.

Thus *each of the three forces may be represented by the part of* AB *intercepted by the directions of the other two.*

The decomposition of a single force into two parallel forces, which shall act in the same sense and satisfy certain conditions, is a very simple application of the foregoing results. Thus, suppose it be required to resolve the given force R into two parallel forces P and Q, one of which (P) is also given. Here, assuming the points A, B and O [Fig. 17], as the points of application of the forces P, Q and R respectively, the given quantities are R, P and OA; and the required quantities, Q and OB. To find Q, we have $R = P + Q$; from which, $Q = R - P$; and to find OB we have

$$Q : P :: \text{OA} : \text{OB};$$

from which

$$\text{OB} = \frac{P}{Q} \times \text{OA} = \frac{P}{R - P} \times \text{OA}.$$

21. We shall now consider the case in which the forces P and Q, applied as before at the extremities of the line AB [Fig. 18], act in opposite senses.

The force Q may be either greater or less than P:

if Q is greater than P, let it be resolved into the two forces P' and R, both acting in the same sense as Q; the first equal to P, and applied at A in the direction of P produced. We have, to determine the intensity of R,

$$Q = P' + R;$$

from which,

$$R = Q - P' = Q - P;$$

and to determine O its point of application, we have

$$R : P' = P :: \text{AB} : \text{OB};$$

from which,

$$\text{OB} = \frac{P}{Q - P} \times \text{AB}.$$

Employing now in place of Q, its two components $P' = P$ and R, the two given forces P and Q may be replaced by the three P, P' and R; of these, P and P' destroying each other, there remains only the force R as the equivalent of the given forces: hence $R = (Q - P)$ applied at the point O, and acting in the same sense as Q, is the resultant sought.

In like manner, it may be shown that if P is greater than Q, the resultant R' is equal to $P - Q$, acting in the same sense as P, and applied at O′ a point situated to the left of A.

Thus when the given forces act in opposite senses, their resultant is situated *without the forces* (not between them, as in the preceding case), *and on the side of the greater, and it acts in the same sense as the greater.*

In this, as in the preceding case, it is evidently true that

$$P : Q : R :: \mathrm{OB} : \mathrm{OA} : \mathrm{AB}.$$

22. If in the value of OB, derived from the proportion

$$P : R :: \mathrm{OB} : \mathrm{AB},$$

we substitute for R its value $(Q - P)$, we get

$$\mathrm{OB} = \frac{P}{Q - P} \times \mathrm{AB}.$$

From this equation, it appears that as the difference between Q and P diminishes, the resultant, constantly diminishing, is applied at a point more and more distant from B, till when $Q = P$ its intensity is reduced to zero, and the distance of the point of application becomes infinite. In this case, therefore, there is really no resultant. Such a system, consisting of two equal and parallel forces acting in opposite senses, but not in the same straight line, is called *a couple.*

23. *Parallel forces not in the same plane.*

Let P, P', P'', etc. be the forces, and let their points of application be A, B, C, etc. [Fig. 19]; the points being so connected by the inflexible straight lines AB, BC, etc. as constantly to retain the same relative positions. Required the intensity of the resultant, and its point of application.

We first compound any two of the forces, as P and P', and find the point M at which their resultant $P + P'$ is applied, by the proportion

$$\mathrm{AB} : \mathrm{AM} :: P + P' : P'.$$

We next compound the resultant $P + P'$ with any one of the remaining forces, as P''; and find the point N at which their resultant $P + P' + P''$ is applied, by the proportion

$$MC : MN :: P + P' + P'' : P''.$$

Proceeding in this manner, constantly compounding the last resultant with one of the remaining forces, we finally arrive at K the point of application of the resultant $R = P + P' + P'' +$ etc. of the whole system. The resultant evidently acts in the same sense as the components, and parallel to their common line of direction.

24. In the case just considered, we have supposed all the forces to act in the same sense. When some of them act in one sense, and some in the opposite sense, *a circumstance indicated by difference of sign*, we find by the preceding method the resultants R' and R'' of the two systems, and their points of application K′ and K″ separately; and then reduce these resultants to a single force R, and find its point of application K by the ordinary rules. When the two resultants are equal, but not directly opposite, the case is that of Art. 22.

25. In determining the point of application of the resultant of the system, we employ only the intensities of the forces, and the mutual distances of their points of application; quantities which are not affected by giving to the directions of the forces a common motion about these points. Hence whatever change we make in the common direction of a

system of parallel forces, applied at points of which the relative positions are invariable, by revolving the directions of the forces about their points of application by a common motion, the point of application of the resultant of the system remains the same. The point of application of the resultant of a system of parallel forces is called *the centre of parallel forces.*

If the centre of parallel forces in any system is a fixed point, the system is evidently in equilibrium *in all positions about that point.*

26. Let us now suppose the points of application of the forces to be referred to three co-ordinate planes, and let us seek the position of the point of application of the resultant, or the centre of parallel forces, with respect to these planes.

Let x, y, z, be the co-ordinates of the point A;
x', y', z', " " " B;
x'', y'', z'', " " " C;
etc.;

and $x_{\prime}, y_{\prime}, z_{\prime}$, the co-ordinates of the centre of parallel forces.

Let E [Fig. 20] be the point of application of the resultant of P and P'; draw AI, EK and BL perpendicular to the plane XOY; join the points I and L, and draw BG parallel to IL. We have [Art. 20]

$$P + P' : P :: \text{AB} : \text{EB}.$$

But the similar triangles AGB, EHB give

$$\text{AB} : \text{EB} :: \text{AG} : \text{EH};$$

hence $P + P' : P :: \text{AG} : \text{EH}$,

and $(P + P')\ \text{EH} = P \times \text{AG}$.

Adding to each member of this equation the product $(P + P')$ HK, we get

$$(P + P')\ (\text{HK} + \text{EH}) = (P + P')\ \text{HK} + P \times \text{AG}$$
$$= P\ (\text{HK} + \text{AG}) + P' \times \text{HK},$$

or $(P + P')\ \text{EK} = P \times \text{AI} + P' \times \text{BL}$;

and denoting the ordinate EK by Z, we have

$$(P + P')\ Z = Pz + P'z'.$$

Compounding the resultant $P + P'$ applied at E, with the third force P'', and denoting the co-ordinate of the point of application of their resultant by Z', we get

$$(P + P' + P'')\ Z' = (P + P')\ Z + P''z'';$$

and substituting for $(P + P')\ Z$ its value $Pz + P'z'$, we have

$$(P + P' + P'')\ Z' = Pz + P'z' + P''z''.$$

Proceeding in the same manner with the remaining forces, and denoting as before the resultant of the system by R, we finally arrive at the equation

$$Rz_{\prime} = Pz + P'z' + P''z'' + P'''z''' + \text{etc.} \quad \ldots\ldots\ldots [9]$$

The first member of this equation is the product of the resultant by the perpendicular let fall from its point of application, upon the plane XOY; and the second member is the sum of the products obtained by multiplying each of the given forces by the perpendicular let fall from its point of application, upon the same plane. These products are called *the moments* of the forces with respect to the plane XOY; thus Rz, Pz, are called *the moments* of R and P respectively referred to this plane. The result contained in this equation may then be thus enunciated: *The moment of the resultant of a system of parallel forces, with respect to any plane whatever, is equal to the sum of the moments of the forces with respect to the same plane.*

Since the forces are affected with the positive or negative sign, according to the sense in which they act, and the signs of the co-ordinates of the points of application are also positive or negative, according to the positions of the points, the signs of the moments, determined by the ordinary rules, may be either positive or negative.

If the moments of the given forces be taken with respect to the planes XOZ, YOZ, we shall get

$$Ry_{\prime} = Py + P'y' + P''y'' + \text{etc.}, \ldots\ldots\ldots\ldots [10]$$

$$Rx_{\prime} = Px + P'x' + P''x'' + \text{etc.}, \ldots\ldots\ldots\ldots [11]$$

and thus we shall have, to determine the centre of parallel forces,

$$x_{\prime} = \frac{Px + P'x' + P''x'' + \text{etc.}}{R},$$

$$y_{\prime} = \frac{Py + P'y' + P''y'' + \text{etc.}}{R},$$

$$z_{\prime} = \frac{Pz + P'z' + P''z'' + \text{etc.}}{R}.$$

27. *If the plane with respect to which the moments are taken, passes through the centre of parallel forces, the sum*

of the moments of the forces is equal to zero; for if we suppose the plane XOY to be that plane, we shall have

$$z_{\prime} = 0,$$

and hence $$Pz + P'z' + P''z'' + \text{etc.} = 0.$$

28. *Parallel forces in the same plane.*

It may happen that the points of application of the forces are all in the same plane: when this is the case, the centre of parallel forces, if it exist, is also situated in this plane, and two co-ordinates are sufficient to determine its position. Thus if we suppose the plane XOY to coincide with this plane, we shall have

$$z = 0, \quad z' = 0, \quad z'' = 0, \text{ etc.},$$

and hence $$z_{\prime} = 0;$$

and the position of the point will be determined by the co-ordinates $x_{\prime}$ and $y_{\prime}$, the values of which are given by equations [10] and [11].

If the points of application are all situated in the same straight line, the centre of parallel forces will also be found in this line, and its position will be determined by a single co-ordinate. Thus if we suppose the axis OX to coincide with this line, we shall have

$$y = 0, \quad y' = 0, \quad y'' = 0, \text{ etc.};$$

$$z = 0, \quad z' = 0, \quad z'' = 0, \text{ etc.};$$

and hence $$y_{\prime} = 0 \text{ and } z_{\prime} = 0,$$

and the value of $x_{\prime}$, given by the equation

$$Rx_{\prime} = Px + P'x' + P''x'' + \text{etc.},$$

will determine the position of the centre of parallel forces with respect to the point O.

29. *Conditions of equilibrium.*

Let the plane XOY [Fig. 21] be taken perpendicular to the direction of the forces; and let the forces be reduced, as in Art. 24, to the partial components R' and R'', applied at the points K′ and K″. The conditions of equilibrium will obviously be,

§ 1. That R' and R'' shall be equal to each other, and act in opposite senses.

§ 2. That their lines of direction shall coincide.

The first condition is expressed by the equation

$$R' = -R''. \qquad \text{[a]}$$

But supposing P, P', P'', etc. to be the components of R', and P''', P^{iv}, P^{v}, etc. to be those of R'', we have

$$R' = P + P' + P'' + \text{etc.},$$

and $$R'' = P''' + P^{\text{iv}} + P^{\text{v}} + \text{etc.}:$$

hence, by substitution, equation [a] becomes

$$P + P' + P'' + P''' + P^{\text{iv}} + P^{\text{v}} + \text{etc.} = 0 \qquad [12]$$

To express the second condition algebraically, let the co-ordinates of K′ and K″, referred to the planes XOZ, YOZ, be denoted by $x_{\prime\prime}$, $y_{\prime\prime}$ and $x_{\prime\prime\prime}$, $y_{\prime\prime\prime}$: then in order that the lines of direction of R' and R'' may coincide, we must evidently have

$$x_{\prime\prime} = x_{\prime\prime\prime} \quad \text{and} \quad y_{\prime\prime} = y_{\prime\prime\prime}.$$

Multiplying these equations by equation [a], we get

$$R'x_{\prime\prime} = -R''x_{\prime\prime\prime}, \qquad \text{[b]}$$

$$R'y_{\prime\prime} = -R''y_{\prime\prime\prime}. \qquad \text{[c]}$$

But by the principle of moments [Art. 26], we have

$$R'x_{,,} = Px + P'x' + P''x'' + \text{etc.},$$
$$R''x_{,,,} = P'''x''' + P^{\text{IV}}x^{\text{IV}} + P^{\text{V}}x^{\text{V}} + \text{etc.};$$
$$R'y_{,,} = Py + P'y' + P''y'' + \text{etc.},$$
$$R''y_{,,,} = P'''y''' + P^{\text{IV}}y^{\text{IV}} + P^{\text{V}}y^{\text{V}} + \text{etc.}$$

Hence equations [b] and [c] become, by substitution,

$$Px + P'x' + P''x'' + P'''x''' + P^{\text{IV}}x^{\text{IV}} + P^{\text{V}}x^{\text{V}} + \text{etc.} = 0, \quad [13]$$
$$Py + P'y' + P''y'' + P'''y''' + P^{\text{IV}}y^{\text{IV}} + P^{\text{V}}y^{\text{V}} + \text{etc.} = 0. \quad [14]$$

Thus when the system is in equilibrium, equations [12], [13] and [14] must be satisfied; and conversely when these equations are satisfied, the system is in equilibrium. These equations express,

§ 1. [Equa. 12] *That the algebraic sum of the forces must be equal to zero.*

§ 2. [Equa. 13 and 14] *That the sum of the moments of the forces, taken with respect to two planes at right angles with each other, and parallel to the common direction of the forces, must also be equal to zero.*

30. When the second of these conditions only is satisfied, that is, when equations [13] and [14] are satisfied, but not equation [12], the given forces will have a resultant, the direction of which will coincide with the intersection of the two planes with respect to which the moments are taken; for since the sum of the moments of the forces is equal to zero with respect to each of the planes, the moments of the resultant with respect to these planes are also equal to zero, and hence the centre of parallel forces must be in each plane; moreover the direction of the re-

sultant is parallel to the planes: consequently the direction of the resultant must coincide with the intersection of the planes.

If there be a fixed point in the intersection of the planes, the resultant will be destroyed, and an equilibrium will exist. Hence *when parallel forces which have a resultant are applied to a system of material points rigidly connected, of which one is fixed, there will be an equilibrium, if the sum of the moments of the forces taken with respect to two planes drawn through the fixed point, parallel to the direction of the forces, and at right angles to each other, is equal to zero.*

We shall next consider the subject of *oblique* forces applied at different points. There are two cases: 1° When the forces act in the same plane; 2° When they act in different planes.

OF OBLIQUE FORCES APPLIED AT DIFFERENT POINTS, AND ACTING IN THE SAME PLANE.

31. Let the intensities of the forces be denoted by P, P', P'', P''', etc.; and let the plane which contains their directions be taken for the co-ordinate plane XOY [Fig. 22]. Let the points A, B, C, D, etc., connected with each other in an invariable manner, be the points of application of the forces as represented in the figure. The resultant of the system, when it exists, may be found in the following manner: Commencing with P and P', any two of the forces, produce their directions till they meet in G. Suppose the two forces applied at this point; and taking G*m*

and Gn to represent their intensities, construct the parallelogram GmG$'n$: the diagonal GG$'$ is their resultant. In like manner, compound the resultant GG$'$ with P'' any one of the remaining forces, transferring their points of application to H their point of meeting, and thus determine their resultant HH$'$. Continue this process till all the forces have been compounded: the last resultant will be the resultant of the system. In the case of the given forces P, P', P'', P''', the resultant is II$'$.

If, in any part of the operation, we arrive at forces of which the directions are parallel, we apply to them the rules for parallel forces.

If, in the final result, we find two equal forces acting in parallel lines and opposite senses, the system has no resultant [Art. 22].

The above method is equivalent to applying the given forces at the point I, in lines parallel to their original directions, and then reducing them to a single force. For the resultant II$'$, applied at I may be resolved into the two forces I$n'' = P'''$ and Im''; Im'' may be resolved into Iu and Iv, equal and parallel to the forces H$n' = P''$ and Hm'; and so on till in place of II$'$ we have all the original forces applied at I, and acting in lines parallel to their primitive directions.

32. The resultant of the forces P, P', P'', P''', etc. may also be determined by the following method: The co-ordinates of the points of application referred to the axes OX, OY being given, and also the angles

which the directions of the forces make with the axes, let each force be resolved into two components parallel to OX and OY respectively. The whole system of forces will thus be resolved into two systems of components, the one parallel to OX, the other parallel to OY. Let these components be applied at the points where their directions intersect the axes, and let the resultants X and Y of the two partial systems be determined in intensity and position by the rules for parallel forces [articles 24 and 28]: the resultant of X and Y, or the resultant of the whole system, may then be determined by the ordinary rule.

Before we proceed to determine the conditions of equilibrium, it is necessary to make known some of the properties of what are called *moments* referred to a point.

Of moments referred to a point.

33. Let P and P' be any two forces meeting in A [Fig. 23], and represented by AB and AC respectively, and let their resultant AD be denoted by R. In the plane of the forces, assume any point O; and from it let fall upon the directions of P, P' and R, the perpendiculars OI, OI′, OI″. Through the points A and O, draw the straight line AO, and through A draw AQ at right angles to AO. Also from the points B, C and D, let fall upon AQ the perpendiculars BD′, CD″, DD‴; and through C draw CE parallel to AQ. The similar triangle AOI, ABD′ give

$$AO : OI :: AB : AD';$$

or, denoting AO and OI by c and p respectively,

$$c : p :: P : \text{AD}';$$

from which we get

$$\text{AD}' = \frac{Pp}{c}.$$

In like manner, denoting by p' and r the perpendiculars OI′ and OI″, and employing the corresponding triangles, we get

$$\text{AD}'' = \frac{P'p'}{c}, \quad \text{AD}''' = \frac{Rr}{c}.$$

But the equal triangles ABD′, CDE give

$$\text{AD}' = \text{CE} = \text{D}''\text{D}''',$$

and hence we have

$$\text{AD}''' = \text{AD}'' + \text{D}''\text{D}'''$$
$$= \text{AD}'' + \text{AD}';$$

and substituting in this equation the values of the several terms found above, we get

$$\frac{Rr}{c} = \frac{Pp}{c} + \frac{P'p'}{c},$$

or

$$Rr = Pp + P'p'. \qquad [15]$$

We have supposed the point O to be taken without the angle BAC, or the opposite vertical angle B′AC′: when it is taken within either of these angles, BAC for example, as in figure 24, we have, as in the preceding case,

$$\text{AD}' = \text{CE} = \text{D}''\text{D}''',$$

and hence $\quad \text{D}'\text{D}''' = \text{AD}''.$

Hence we have

$$\text{AD}''' = \text{AD}' - \text{D}'\text{D}''' = \text{AD}' - \text{AD}'';$$

and substituting as above, we get

$$Rr = Pp - P'p'. \quad\ldots\ldots\ldots\ldots\ldots\ldots [16]$$

The products Rr, Pp, etc. are called *the moments of the forces* R, P, etc. with respect to the assumed point O; and the point itself is called *the centre of moments.* Thus *the moment of a force with respect to a point, is the product of the force by the perpendicular let fall from the point upon the direction of the force.* Employing these terms, the principle involved in equations [15] and [16] may be thus enunciated:

The moment of the resultant of any two forces is equal to the sum or difference of the moments of the forces, according as the centre of moments is taken without or within the angle made by the directions of the forces, or the opposite angle at the vertex made by their directions produced.

Another enunciation of this principle may be given by introducing the idea of motion. Thus, suppose the perpendiculars OI, OI′, OI″, to be inflexible lines, capable of motion in the plane of the forces, about the point O regarded as a fixed point: then the forces P, P' and R, which we may imagine applied at the points I, I′ and I″, will tend to give to the perpendiculars a motion of rotation about O; and we perceive that in figure 23, in which the centre of moments is without the angle BAC, or its opposite angle at the vertex, these forces will tend to turn their points of application in the same sense about O: while, on the contrary, in figure 24, in which the centre of moments is within one of these angles, the two components will tend to turn their points of application in opposite senses about O, and the resultant will tend to turn its point of application in the same sense as the component which has the greater moment. We may therefore say that *the moment of the resultant of any two forces is equal to the sum or difference of the moments of the forces, according as the forces tend to turn their points of application in the same sense, or in opposite senses, about the fixed point assumed in their plane as the centre of moments.*

34. This principle can be shown to be true, whatever the number of forces. Let us consider the case in which the centre of moments is so situated that the first three of the forces P, P', P'', P''', etc. tend to turn the system in one sense, and the remaining forces in the opposite sense about that point. Let Q be the resultant of P and P', and Q' that of Q and P''. Also let p, p', p'', q and q', denote the perpendiculars let fall from the centre of moments on the directions of P, P', P'', Q and Q' respectively. Then, according to the principle just demonstrated, we shall have

$$Qq = Pp + P'p',$$

$$Q'q' = Qq + P''p'';$$

and substituting in the second of these equations the value of Qq derived from the first, we shall get

$$Q'q' = Pp + P'p' + P''p''.$$

Again, denoting by $Q_{,}$ the resultant of the remaining

forces P''', P^{IV}, etc.; by $q_{,}$ the perpendicular let fall from the centre of moments upon its direction; and by p''', p^{IV}, etc. the perpendiculars drawn from the same point to the directions of P''', P^{IV}, etc., we shall have

$$Q_{,}q_{,} = P'''p''' + P^{IV}p^{IV} + \text{etc.}$$

Let now the resultant of Q' and $Q_{,}$ (that is, the resultant of the given forces P, P', P'', etc.) be denoted by R, and the perpendicular let fall from the centre of moments upon its direction by r. Moreover let it be recollected that Q' and $Q_{,}$ tend to turn their points of application in opposite directions. Then, according as $Q'q'$ is greater or less than $Q_{,}q_{,}$, we shall have, since Rr must be positive,

$$Rr = Q'q' - Q_{,}q_{,},$$

or

$$Rr = Q_{,}q_{,} - Q'q'.$$

In the first case, the force R will tend to turn the system in the same sense as the force Q', and consequently in the same sense as the forces P, P' and P''. Supposing this to be the case in question, and substituting for $Q'q'$, $Q_{,}q_{,}$, the values found above, we get

$$Rr = Pp + P'p' + P''p'' - P'''p''' - P^{IV}p^{IV} - \text{etc.} \ldots\ldots [17]$$

Thus, whatever the number of forces, *the moment of the resultant is equal to the sum of the moments of the forces which tend to turn the system in the same sense as the resultant, minus the sum of the moments of the forces which tend to turn it in the opposite sense.*

35. If, in the plane of a system of forces such as we have been considering, there is a fixed point with which the points of application are connected, and about which they may revolve in the plane of the system, the forces will obviously be in equilibrium if their resultant passes through this point. Suppose their resultant thus to pass, and take the fixed point for the centre of moments; then we shall have

$$r = 0,$$

and hence $$Rr = 0,$$

and equation [17] will become

$$Pp + P'p' + P''p'' + \text{etc.} = 0.$$

Hence, in order to an equilibrium in this case, it is only necessary that the sum of the moments of the forces which tend to turn the system in one sense about the fixed point, should be equal to the sum of the moments of the forces which tend to turn the system in the opposite sense, the moments being taken with respect to the fixed point.

36. If, in the case of a system of forces P, P', P'', etc. in which there is a resultant, that is, in which R is not equal to zero, we have

$$Pp + P'p' + P''p'' + \text{etc.} = 0,$$

then $$Rr = 0,$$

and hence $$r = 0,$$

and consequently the resultant passes through the point assumed as the centre of moments.

37. *Conditions of equilibrium.*

Let P, P' and P'' be any three forces situated in the same plane, and applied at the points A, B and C, as represented in figure 25. It is essential to an equilibrium, that their directions should meet in the same point; for in order that any two of them, as P and P', may be in equilibrium with the third P'', the latter must act in the same line with the resultant R of the two former, and hence its direction must pass through the point A at which the directions of P and P' intersect. But P may be supposed to be the resultant of two other forces P''' and P^{IV}, applied at the point E, as in the figure; P^{IV}, of two others P^{V} and P^{VI}, and so on. Hence in order that any number of forces situated in the same plane, and applied at different points, may be in equilibrium, they must be reducible to three forces which meet in the same point. To express this condition algebraically, let the forces P, P' and P'' be supposed to be applied at A [Fig. 26] their point of meeting, and let their intensities be represented by AB, AC and $AD_{\prime\prime}$, $AD_{\prime}$ being equal to AD or R the resultant of P and P'. Also from a point O assumed in the plane of the forces, let the lines OI, OI′, OI″, be drawn perpendicular to the directions of P, P' and P'' or R. Recurring to article 33, and employing the same notation as in that article, we perceive that the relation between these forces and perpendiculars is expressed by the equation

$$Rr = Pp \pm P'p',$$

or, substituting for Rr its equal $P''p''$, by the equation

$$P''p'' = Pp \pm P'p' \; ; \ldots\ldots\ldots\ldots\ldots\ldots \text{[a]}$$

the upper or lower sign of the second member being employed, according to the position of the point O.

This equation expresses that the moment of the force which tends to turn the system in one sense about the centre of moments, is equal to the sum of the moments of the forces which tend to turn it in the opposite sense; and a little consideration renders it apparent that when this condition is fulfilled, the forces P, P' and P'' must meet in the same point. Equation [a] may therefore be taken for the equation of condition in the case of three forces, the forces necessarily meeting in the same point when it is satisfied. To deduce from it the equation for a greater number of forces, let P be considered as the resultant of the two forces P''' and P^{IV}, applied at some point E taken in the direction of P: we shall have, by the principle of moments,

$$Pp = P'''\,p''' - P^{\text{IV}}p^{\text{IV}},$$

(it being supposed, as represented in the figure, that P''' and P^{IV} tend to turn their points of application in opposite senses about the point O, P and P''' in the same sense;) and substituting this value of Pp in equation [a], and employing the upper sign of the second member, we shall get

$$P''p'' = P'''p''' - P^{\text{IV}}p^{\text{IV}} + P'p',$$

or

$$P''p'' + P^{\text{IV}}p^{\text{IV}} = P'p' + P'''p''',$$

for the equation of condition in the case of four forces. By thus successively regarding one of the forces as the resultant of two others, the equation of condition may be found for any number of forces. The general equation is commonly written thus,

$$Pp + P'p' + P''p'' + P'''p''' + \text{etc.} = 0\,;$$

the signs of the terms being determined by the directions in which the several forces tend to turn their points of application.

Since this equation indicates that the forces P, P', P'', P''', etc. are reducible to three forces which meet in the same point, when it is satisfied, we may suppose all the forces applied at the point of meeting of the three forces in lines parallel to their primitive directions. The conditions of equilibrium will thus be reduced to those of article 15; and adopting the notation of that article, we shall have for the remaining equations of condition,

$$P\cos a + P'\cos a' + P''\cos a'' + P'''\cos a''' + \text{etc.} = 0,$$

$$P\cos\beta + P'\cos\beta' + P''\cos\beta'' + P'''\cos\beta''' + \text{etc.} = 0.$$

Thus the equations of condition for the equilibrium of any number of forces situated in the same plane, and applied at different points, are

$$\Sigma\,(P\cos a) = 0, \quad\ldots\ldots\ldots\ldots\ldots\ldots\ldots [18]$$

$$\Sigma\,(P\cos\beta) = 0, \quad\ldots\ldots\ldots\ldots\ldots\ldots\ldots [19]$$

$$\Sigma\,(Pp) \quad = 0. \quad\ldots\ldots\ldots\ldots\ldots\ldots\ldots [20]$$

OF FORCES APPLIED AT DIFFERENT POINTS, AND SITUATED IN DIFFERENT PLANES.

38. This is the most general case: We shall not discuss it in detail, but merely indicate the principal steps in the several processes.

The forces being given in intensity, direction, and the position of the points of application (these points being conceived to be rigidly connected as in the preceding case), to determine their resultant, when it exists, we proceed as follows:

1° We reduce the given system to two partial systems (b) and (c): the one consisting of forces situated in the plane of xy;* the other, of forces perpendicular to that plane, and hence parallel to the axis of z.

2° By the foregoing methods [Articles 32 and 23], we determine the resultants of the systems (b) and (c).

3° When these resultants are situated in the same plane, we reduce them to a single force by the ordinary rule.

If the resultants are not situated in the same plane, the given forces are obviously not reducible to a single force.

39. *Conditions of equilibrium.*

If the systems (b) and (c) are separately in equilibrium, the given system must evidently be in equilibrium. The converse is also true, viz. that if the given system is in equilibrium, the systems (b) and

* The position of the co-ordinate planes being arbitrary, we may give to the plane of xy any position whatever.

(c) must be separately in equilibrium. For if an equilibrium exists among the given forces, it will evidently not be destroyed by supposing any line of the plane of xy, connected with the points of application, to become immovable; but in this case, the forces situated in the plane of xy will be destroyed by the resistance of the fixed line; and hence the forces parallel to the axis of z, unless in equilibrium amongst themselves, will tend to turn the plane about this line: therefore, since the equilibrium must continue, the forces parallel to the axis of z must destroy each other. The system [c] being thus necessarily in equilibrium of itself, the system [b] must be also. The conditions of equilibrium for these systems have already been found [articles 29 and 37]; those for the system [b] are expressed by the equations [18], [19] and [20]; those for the system [c] by the equations [12], [13] and [14].

40. When the system contains a fixed line, about which the points of application may revolve, without being capable of moving in a direction parallel to it (in the same manner as the material points of a solid body about an axis on which the body is prevented from sliding), the conditions of equilibrium can be expressed by a single equation. This case of equilibrium, being one to which we shall have to refer hereafter, we will treat it more fully than we have treated the preceding case.

Let OZ [Fig. 27] be the fixed line or axis, about which the points of application may revolve in the manner just supposed, and let it be taken for the axis of z. Let AK be the direction of any one of the forces, as P, and A its point of application. Through AK let a plane be drawn perpendicular to the plane of xy; and let P, represented by AK, be decomposed in this plane into the two forces AH and AG, the one parallel to the plane of xy, the other parallel to the axis of z. Since the point A can by hypothesis have no motion parallel to the axis of z, the second component must be destroyed. The first, which we will denote by Q, is expended in tending to give to the point A a motion of rotation about the axis. We will now show that this force may be replaced by another, equal and parallel to it, but applied in the plane of xy. For this purpose, let the line GA be produced to meet the plane of xy in A′; and through A′, let the line A′H′ be drawn parallel to AH. Also through the axis OZ, let the plane ON′NN″ be drawn perpendicular to the parallels AH, A′H′, and meeting these parallels produced in N and N′. Without affecting the system, we may apply at the point A′ two forces S and S', each equal to Q, and acting in the opposite directions A′H′, A′E; thus replacing the force Q by the forces S, S' and Q. But conceiving the plane ON′NN″ to be rigidly connected with the points of application, the forces Q and S', which we may suppose applied at N and N′, and which tend to turn this plane in opposite directions, will, as we shall presently show, destroy each other by means of the fixed axis; and we shall have, as the equivalent of Q, only the force S, equal and parallel to Q, and acting in the same sense as it. Each force of the system is capable of a similar reduction. Thus the given forces P, P', P'', etc., applied at the points A, B, C, etc., may be replaced by the components Q, Q', Q'', etc., $Q_{,}$, $Q_{,,}$, $Q_{,,,}$ etc., applied at determinate points of the plane xy. Hence since the point O is fixed, in order to an equilibrium, it is only necessary that the sum of the moments of the forces which tend to turn the system in one sense, may be equal to the sum of the moments of the forces which tend to turn it in the opposite sense about the point O taken as the centre of moments. If then we denote the perpendiculars drawn from O to the directions of the forces, by q, q', q'', etc., $q_{,}$, $q_{,,}$, $q_{,,,}$ etc. respectively, and suppose that the forces Q, Q', Q'', etc. tend to turn the system in one sense, and $Q_{,}$, $Q_{,,}$, $Q_{,,,}$ etc. in the opposite sense, we shall have for the equation of condition,

$$Qq + Q'q' + \text{etc.} - Q_{,}q_{,} - Q_{,,}q_{,,} - \text{etc.} = 0 \ldots\ldots\ldots [21]$$

To show that the forces Q and S' are in equilibrium with each other, by means of the fixed axis, at the points O and N'', let the forces S'' and S''', S^{IV} and S^{V} be applied, each equal and parallel to Q; S'' and S^{IV} acting in the same sense as Q, S''' and S^{V} in the opposite sense. These forces will obviously not change the state of the system; and hence we may consider the two forces Q and S' as replaced by the six forces Q and S'', S' and S^{V}, S''' and S^{IV}. But of these, Q and S'', S' and S^{v}, may be reduced to two equal and opposite forces applied at I the point of intersection of the diagonals ON, N′N″, and are therefore in equilibrium; and the remaining forces S''' and S^{iv}, acting upon the fixed points O and N″, are destroyed by the reaction of the points. Consequently the six forces are in equilibrium by means of the fixed axis, and hence the equivalent system Q and S' must also be in equilibrium.

CENTRE OF GRAVITY.

41. The force which causes a body, when not supported, to fall to the earth, is called *gravity*. We learn from experiment, 1° That gravity acts with equal intensity upon the particles of all bodies, however the bodies may differ in size, form, or nature; 2° That it acts in directions perpendicular to the surface of the earth, or the surface of a liquid at rest.

The line of direction of gravity at any place, is called *the vertical* at that place; and any plane perpendicular to the vertical, is called *a horizontal plane*.

Since the form of the earth is nearly spherical, the directions of gravity at different points will converge towards its centre; but the length of the earth's radius is so great, compared with the dimensions of the bodies usually treated of in mechanics, that we may neglect this convergence, and consider the directions of gravity, for all the points of the same body, as parallel.

From experiments and observations which will be made known hereafter, it has been found,

1° That the intensity of gravity at the surface of the earth, though always the same at the same place, varies with the latitude of the place; being least at the equator, and increasing as we approach the poles, in the ratio of the square of the sine of the latitude.

2° That its intensity varies from one point to another of the same vertical; diminishing as the distance of the point from the centre of the earth increases, in the ratio of the square of the distance.

But the variations of intensity from these two causes, for small changes of distance, are so minute that the action of gravity upon all the particles of a body of ordinary size may be considered as equally intense. Since then within the requisite limits, gravity may be considered as constant in both intensity and direction, we may regard the particles of a heavy body as the points of application of a system of equal and parallel forces, acting vertically and in the same sense. The resultant of these forces, which is equal to their sum, and presses the body vertically downwards, will evidently constitute what is called *the weight* of the body. If then we denote the weight of the body by W; the number of material particles composing it, by M; and the effect of gravity upon a single particle, by g, we shall have

$$W = Mg \qquad [22]$$

An immediate inference from this equation is, that in homogeneous bodies, the weights are proportional to the volumes; a deduction constantly verified by experiment.

In heterogeneous bodies, this relation between the weights and volumes does not hold; the weights of equal volumes, when compared, being found unequal. Thus a cubic inch of gold is found to weigh about nineteen times as much as a cubic inch of distilled water at a certain standard temperature; a cubic inch of silver, eleven times as much.

Since the weights of equal volumes of two substances must be directly as the numbers of material particles which they contain, equal volumes of gold and silver must contain, the one nineteen, the other eleven times as many material particles as the same volume of distilled water. Thus the numbers 19 and 11 express the relative numbers of material particles, or the relative quantities of matter contained in equal volumes of gold and silver; the number of particles, or the quantity of matter, in an equal volume of water, being assumed as the unit. The numbers which thus express the relative quantities of matter referred to a common unit, contained in equal volumes of heterogeneous bodies, are called the densities of these bodies; thus 19 and 11 are the densities of gold and silver respectively, the density of distilled water being taken for the unit. If now we denote the density of a body by D; its volume, expressed in terms of the unit of volume, by V; and the number of particles that it contains, that is, its quantity of matter, or *mass*, by M, we shall evidently have

$$M = VD. \quad \text{[23]}$$

If we substitute this value of M in equation [22], we shall get

$$W = VDg. \quad \text{[24]}$$

Since the value of g the general symbol denoting the intensity of gravity, varies with the position of the place, we take its value at some determinate place for the unit of intensity, and consider its general value as expressed in terms of this unit. We thus have for the place at which $g = 1$,

$$W = VD;$$

and for any place whatever,

$$W = VDg,$$

g being in this equation the ratio of the intensities of gravity at the two places. If the unit of volume be the cubic inch, the unit of weight is evidently the weight of a cubic inch of distilled water at the place where $g = 1$, and W designates the number of these units which the weight of the body contains.

42. Since the weight of a body is the resultant of a system of parallel forces applied at points of which the relative positions are fixed, it must have a determinate point of application. This point, which is the centre of parallel forces for the case in question, is called *the centre of gravity* of the body. The position of the centre of gravity, with respect to the

points of the body, is invariable; remaining the same, while we suppose the body to take all possible positions in space; for a change in the position of the body is merely equivalent to a revolution of the directions of the forces about their points of application, an operation which [Art. 25] does not affect the position of the centre of parallel forces.

When the centre of gravity of a body is supported, the body will be in equilibrium in all positions about that point; for, in all positions, the direction of the weight of the body will pass through the point of support.

43. Conceive a body now to be divided into any number of parts, and suppose the weights and centres of gravity of the several parts to be known. Let the weights of the parts be denoted by w, w', w'', etc., and the co-ordinates of their centres of gravity by x, y and z; x', y', and z'; x'', y'' and z'', etc. respectively; and let the weight of the entire body be denoted by W, and the co-ordinates of its centre of gravity by $x_{,}$, $y_{,}$ and $z_{,}$. Then since W is the resultant of the parallel forces w, w', w'', etc. applied at the respective centres of gravity, we shall have [Art. 26] to determine the co-ordinates $x_{,}$, $y_{,}$, $z_{,}$, the equations

$$\left.\begin{aligned} x_{,} &= \frac{wx + w'x' + w''x'' + \text{etc.}}{W}, \\ y_{,} &= \frac{wy + w'y' + w''y'' + \text{etc.}}{W}, \\ z_{,} &= \frac{wz + w'z' + w''z'' + \text{etc.}}{W}. \end{aligned}\right\} \quad \ldots\ldots\ldots\ldots [25]$$

When the centres of gravity of the several parts are situated in the same plane, the plane of xy for example, the centre of gravity of the entire body will be found in that plane: when they are situated in the same straight line, as the axis of x, it will be found in that line [Art. 28].

The above equations are evidently true, whatever the number of parts into which we suppose the body divided.

44. If we denote the masses corresponding to the weights W, w, w', w'', etc. by M, m, m', m'', etc., we shall have

$$W = Mg, \quad w = mg, \quad w' = m'g, \quad w'' = m''g, \text{ etc.};$$

and by substituting these values in the above equations, and omitting the common factor g, we shall get

$$\left.\begin{aligned} x_{\prime} &= \frac{mx + m'x' + m''x'' + \text{etc.}}{M}, \\ y_{\prime} &= \frac{my + m'y' + m''y'' + \text{etc.}}{M}, \\ z_{\prime} &= \frac{mz + m'z' + m''z'' + \text{etc.}}{M}. \end{aligned}\right\} \quad \ldots\ldots\ldots\ldots [26]$$

From these equations, it appears that the position of the centre of gravity is independent of the intensity of gravity.

45. If we suppose the body to be homogeneous, and denote its volume and density by V and D respectively, and the volumes of its several parts by v, v', v'', etc., we shall have

$$M = VD, \quad m = vD, \quad m' = v'D, \quad m'' = v''D;$$

and by substituting these values in equations [26], and omitting the common factor D, we shall get

$$\left.\begin{aligned} x_{,} &= \frac{vx + v'x' + v''x'' + \text{etc.}}{V}, \\ y_{,} &= \frac{vy + v'y' + v''y'' + \text{etc.}}{V}, \\ z_{,} &= \frac{vz + v'z' + v''z'' + \text{etc.}}{V}. \end{aligned}\right\} \quad \ldots\ldots\ldots\ldots [27]$$

If we suppose the parts into which the body is conceived to be divided, to be infinitely small, we may derive from equations [26] and [27] the following theorem: *The sum of the products obtained by multiplying either the masses or the volumes of the elements, or infinitely small parts of a body, by their respective distances from any plane whatever, is equal to the product of the entire mass or volume by the distance of its centre of gravity from the same plane.*

If the elements of the body are all situated in the same plane, or, in other words, if the body itself is a material plane, we may consider the plane with respect to which the moments are taken as reduced to its line of intersection with the plane of the elements, the two planes being supposed to be perpendicular to each other, and the moments may be supposed to be taken with respect to this line.

It will be recollected that these products, or *moments* of the masses or volumes, as they may be called, must be affected with opposite signs, according as the perpendiculars are situated on the same or opposite sides of the plane or line.

It is obvious, that if in any case the sum of the moments of the masses or volumes, with respect to the plane or line, is equal to zero, the centre of gravity of the entire body must be situated in the plane or line.

46. *Determination of the centres of gravity of particular bodies.*

The application of the preceding equations to the determination of the centres of gravity of particular bodies, requires in general the use of the integral calculus. In very many cases, however, these points can be determined by the most elementary processes. The examples which follow will illustrate the methods commonly employed.

We shall first consider some of the simplest cases of material or physical lines and surfaces: the lines being conceived to consist of single series of material particles; the surfaces, of single laminæ of particles, the particles being supposed in both cases to be uniformly distributed.

1° *The straight line.*

The centre of gravity of a material straight line is its middle point. For, drawing through this point any line or axis whatever, the sum of the moments of the particles on one side of the axis is obviously equal to the sum of the moments of the particles on the opposite side; and these sums are, moreover, affected with opposite signs. Their algebraic sum is therefore equal to zero, and hence the centre of gravity of the line must, by the last paragraph of the preceding article, be in the axis; but it is also in the line itself, consequently it must be at the point of intersection of the line and the axis.

The same result may be found more directly by applying the ordinary rule for parallel forces. Thus, let the weights of the particles be regarded as a system of equal and parallel forces acting in pairs, the components of each pair being applied on opposite sides of the middle point and at equal distances from it, and let the point of application of the resultant of the whole system be sought. The resultant of each pair, and hence the resultant of the whole system, will be found to pass through the middle point of the line.

2○ *The perimeter of a polygon.*

To determine the centre of gravity of the perimeter of a polygon: in the plane of the polygon, draw the co-ordinate axes OX and OY, and determine the co-ordinates of the centres of gravity of the several sides referred to these axes. Then in the first two of equations [27] Art. 45, substitute for the volumes v, v', v'', etc. the lengths of the sides; for x and y, x' and y', x'' and y'', etc. the co-ordinates of their centres of gravity respectively; and for the volume V, the entire perimeter of the polygon. The values of $x_{,}$ and $y_{,}$, thus determined, will be the values of the co-ordinates of the centre of gravity of the polygon.

Another method consists in regarding the weights of the several sides, applied at the respective centres of gravity, as a system of parallel forces, and determining the point of application of the resultant by the ordinary rule.

3° *The arc of a circle.*

Let AFB [Fig. 28] be an arc of a circle, and let MN be one of the infinitely small parts or particles of which we suppose it made up. Draw the diameter LR parallel to the chord AB; and from Q the middle point of MN, draw QP perpendicular to LR. Draw also the radius QO, the line MI parallel to AB, and the lines MH and NK perpendicular to AB. The similar triangles MNI and QOP give

$$MN : MI :: QO : QP,$$

or

$$MN \times QP = MI \times QO$$

$$= HK \times QO.$$

The first member of this equation is the moment of MN with respect to LR; and the second is the product of the projection of MN on the chord AB, by the radius of the circle. Thus the moment of each particle of the arc is equal to the product of its projection on the chord, by the radius of the circle: consequently the sum of the moments of all the particles of the arc with respect to LR, is equal to the product of the chord by the radius, or to AB × OQ. But the sum of the moments of the particles of the arc, with respect to the radius OF drawn to its middle point, is evidently equal to zero, and hence OF must contain the centre of gravity of the arc. If then we suppose the centre of gravity to be at C, the expression of the moment of the arc with respect to LR will be, arc AFB × CO; and hence [Art. 45] we shall have

$$\text{arc AFB} \times \text{CO} = \text{AB} \times \text{OQ},$$

or $$\text{arc AFB} : \text{AB} :: \text{OQ} : \text{CO}.$$

Hence *the centre of gravity of the arc of a circle is on the radius which bisects the arc, at a point, the distance of which from the centre of the circle is a fourth proportional to the length of the arc, its chord, and radius.*

4° *The area of a parallelogram.*

The centre of gravity of the area of a parallelogram is at the intersection of its diagonals. For the sum of the moments of the particles of the parallelogram, with respect to each of its diagonals, is evidently equal to zero, and hence each diagonal must pass through its centre of gravity: consequently the centre of gravity of the parallelogram must be at the intersection of these lines.

Another method of determining the centres of gravity of plane figures, consists in regarding them as made up of physical lines. To apply this to the case of the parallelogram, conceive it made up of lines parallel to one of its diagonals; the other diagonal, bisecting these parallels, and hence passing through their centres of gravity, will contain the centre of gravity of the entire figure; but this property is common to the two diagonals: consequently the centre of gravity of the parallelogram must be at their intersection.

5°. *The area of a triangle.*

To find the centre of gravity of a triangle ABD [Fig. 29]: From the vertices B and D draw the lines DE and BF to the middle points of the opposite sides AB and AD, and join the points E and F; the centre of gravity will be at C. For, regarding the triangle as made up of physical lines parallel to AB, its centre of gravity must be in the line DE which bisects these parallels: it must also be in BF, which bisects the lines drawn parallel to AD; consequently it is at the point C.

To determine the position of this point, we have, from the similar triangles BCD and FCE, ABD and AEF,

$$\text{CD} : \text{CE} :: \text{BD} : \text{EF}$$
$$:: \text{AB} : \text{AE}$$
$$:: 2 : 1;$$

hence
$$2\,\text{CE} = \text{CD},$$
$$3\,\text{CE} = \text{ED},$$

and
$$\text{CE} = \frac{\text{ED}}{3}.$$

Hence *the centre of gravity of the area of a triangle is on the straight line drawn from any one of its vertices, to the middle point of the opposite side, at a distance from this point equal to one-third of the length of the line.*

6°. *The area of a polygon.*

To determine the centre of gravity of the area of a polygon, divide the polygon into triangles, and find the centre of gravity of each triangle by the preceding method; then proceed as in the case of the perimeter.

7°. *The area of a circular sector.*

Let AOB [Fig. 30] be a circular sector, and let it be supposed to be divided into an infinite number of infinitely small equal triangles, having their bases in AB, and their vertices at the centre O. The centre of gravity of each of these triangles will be in the radius drawn to the middle of its base, at a distance from the centre of the circle equal to two-thirds of the length of the radius: hence the centre of gravity of the sector will be the same as that of the arc FG described with a radius OI, equal to two-thirds the radius of the sector. It will therefore [No. 3° of this Art.] be on the radius OD drawn to the middle of the arc AB, at a point C, the distance of which from O will be given by the proportion

$$\text{arc FIG} : \text{FG} :: \text{OI} : \text{OC};$$

or,

$$\text{arc ADB} : \text{AB} :: \tfrac{2}{3}\text{OD} : \text{OC}.$$

Hence *the centre of gravity of the area of a circular sector is on the radius which bisects the arc of the sector, at a point, the distance of which from the centre is a fourth proportional to the arc, its chord, and two-thirds of the radius.*

8°. *The surface of a spherical zone.*

The centre of gravity of the surface of a spherical zone is at the middle point of its axis, or the line joining the centres of its bases. For, conceive the entire zone divided into an infinite number of infinitely small zones of the same altitude, by planes parallel to its bases;

the centres of gravity of these infinitesimal zones will be on the axis of the entire zone; but these zones are equivalent in surface: hence their common centre of gravity, or the centre of gravity of the entire zone, will be at the middle point of the axis.

9° *The parallelopipedon.*

Let AH [Fig. 31] be a parallelopipedon. Through the opposite edges BG and EI, AF and DH, let the planes BGIE, ADHF be drawn; and through C the middle point of OO′ the intersection of these planes, let the plane A′B′D′E′ be drawn at right angles to OO′.

The matter of the solid is obviously so disposed on the opposite sides of these planes, that the sum of the moments of its particles with respect to each plane is equal to zero: consequently the centre of gravity of the parallelopipedon is at C the common point of intersection of the three planes. This point is obviously the middle point of one of the diagonals of the solid.

Another method of determining the centre of gravity of solids, consists in regarding them as made up of physical planes. Thus, in the case just considered, we may suppose the solid made up of planes parallel to its base ABDE: *the centre of gravity will obviously be at* C *the middle of the line* OO′ *which joins the centres of gravity of the two bases.*

10° *The pyramid.*

Let A – BED [Fig. 32] be a triangular pyramid.

From the vertices A and D, draw to F the middle point of the edge BE, the straight lines AF and DF; take FK equal to one-third of AF, and FH equal to one-third of FD, and draw DK and AH: the point C in which DK and AH intersect is the centre of gravity of the pyramid. For, conceive the pyramid to be made up of planes parallel to the face BED: the line AH will pass through the centres of gravity of all these planes, and will therefore contain the centre of gravity of the pyramid. In like manner it may be shown that the line DK will also contain this point; consequently it must be at C the point of intersection of these lines. To determine its position, joining the points H and K, we have, from the similar triangles ACD, HCK, AFD, KFH,

$$\mathrm{CH} : \mathrm{CA} :: \mathrm{HK} : \mathrm{DA}$$
$$:: \mathrm{FH} : \mathrm{FD}$$
$$:: 1 : 3;$$

hence $$3\mathrm{CH} = \mathrm{CA},$$
$$4\mathrm{CH} = \mathrm{AH},$$

and $$\mathrm{CH} = \frac{\mathrm{AH}}{4}.$$

Hence the centre of gravity of a triangular pyramid is on the straight line drawn from the vertex of any one of its angles, to the centre of gravity of the opposite face, and at a distance from the face equal to one-fourth of the length of the line.

It can now be easily shown that *the centre of gravity of any pyramid whatever is on the straight line drawn from its vertex to the centre of gravity of its base, at a distance from the base equal to one-fourth the length of the line.*

Let A – BDE.... [Fig. 33] be the pyramid. From the vertex A, draw the straight line AI to I the centre of gravity of the base; and divide the base into triangles, by joining its vertices with the point I. From the centres of gravity of the triangles, draw lines to the vertex; and taking IC equal to one-fourth of AI, through C draw a plane parallel to the base of the polygon. The point C will be the centre of gravity of the pyramid. For, since the plane drawn through C cuts all the lines drawn from A to the base proportionally, it will contain the centres of gravity of the triangular pyramids A – IBD, A – IDE, etc., and consequently will also contain the centre of gravity of the entire pyramid; and since the straight line AI passes through the centres of gravity of all the planes drawn parallel to the base, it also will contain the centre of gravity of the entire pyramid: therefore the centre of gravity of the entire pyramid will be at the intersection of the line and plane.

The result just obtained, being independent of the number of sides of the base of the pyramid, is true when the number becomes infinite, and the base a re-entering curve: it is therefore true for a cone of any base whatever.

Any polyhedron being divisible into pyramids, its centre of gravity may be found by conceiving it to be thus divided, and determining the centre of gravity of each pyramid thus formed, with respect to three co-ordinate planes, and then applying equations [27] of article 45.

11° *The spherical sector.*

*The centre of gravity of a spherical sector, or the solid generated by the revolution of a circular sector about one of its sides, is on the axis of the sector, at a distance from the centre of the sphere equal to three-fourths of the radius, minus three-eighths of the altitude or axis of the corresponding spherical calotte.**

For conceive the entire sector to be made up of an infinite number of infinitely small equivalent pyramids, having their vertices at the centre of the sphere. The centre of gravity of each of the pyramids will be on the radius drawn to the centre of gravity of its base, at a distance from the centre of the sphere equal to three-fourths of the radius. The centre of gravity of the entire sector will therefore be the same as that of a spherical calotte concentric with the calotte of the sector, and having its radius equal to three-fourths the radius of the sphere: hence the centre of gravity of the entire sector will be at the middle point of the axis of this concentric calotte. If we denote the height of the calotte of the sector by h, the height of the concentric calotte will be $\frac{3}{4}h$: hence, denoting the radius of the sphere by r, the distance of the centre of gravity of the entire sector from the centre of the sphere will be $\frac{3}{4}r - \frac{3}{8}h$.

* "Spherical *calotte*," or "cap," a spherical zone of one base.

MACHINES.

47. A *machine* is an instrument, by means of which a force may be made to act upon points that lie without its direction.

The *simple machines*, of which all others are composed, are the *cord* or *rope machine*, the *lever*, and the *inclined plane*. Certain modifications or combinations of these are frequently ranked among the simple machines, viz. the *pulley*, the *wheel and axle*, the *screw*, and the *wedge*.

The force employed in working a machine, is called the *power;* and the force to be overcome, the *resistance.*

In discussing the theory of machines, we seek only the conditions of equilibrium of the power and resistance. The consideration of the motion which ensues when the power is increased beyond what is required for an equilibrium, belongs to dynamics.

In the first investigations, we omit the consideration of the weight of the machine, the stiffness of cords, the flexibility of rods, friction, etc. etc.

THE ROPE MACHINE.

48. The simplest form of the rope machine is that represented in figure [34], in which three cords AB, AC and AD, lying in the same plane, are firmly united at a point A; and the forces P, Q and R are applied at their extremities B, C and D. The conditions of equilibrium, in this case, are evidently expressed by the proportion [Art. 12],

$$P : Q : R :: \sin p : \sin q : \sin r; \ldots\ldots [28]$$

p, q and r denoting the angles made by the cords, or the directions of the forces as represented in the figure.

49. If the forces P and Q be suppressed, and the extremities B and C be attached to fixed points, the conditions of equilibrium will still be given by proportion [28]; and P and Q will, in this case, denote the re-actions of the points respectively.

50. When the extremities B and C are fixed, and the cord AD is attached to a ring which is capable of moving freely upon BAC, it is evident, that as the ring slides along this line, the point A will describe an ellipse. Consequently in order to an equilibrium, the direction of AD must coincide with the normal to the curve at the point A, and hence must bisect the angle BAC of the radii vectores. We shall then have

$$p = q \text{ and } P = Q,$$

and $$P : R :: \sin p : \sin r.$$

51. The common intensity of two equal and opposite forces applied at the extremities of a cord, in the direction of its length, so as to extend it, is called the *tension* of the cord; thus, P, Q and R are the tensions of the cords AB, AC and AD respectively. The effect upon the cord will obviously be the same, whether the two equal forces thus act at its extremities, or one of them be suppressed, and the extremity to which it was applied be attached to a fixed point.

52. The case in which there is any number of cords united at the same point, and solicited by forces lying in the same plane, is immediately reducible to that just considered.

53. Another form of this machine, called the *funicular polygon*, is represented in figure [35]; in which EABCF, AG, BH, CI, are supposed to be cords united at the points A, B and C, and solicited at their extremities by the forces P, P', P'', etc. acting in the same plane. When these forces are in equilibrium with each other, it can readily be shown:

1°. That the forces must be such that they will be in equilibrium when applied at a single point (C, for example, as represented in the figure), parallel to their primitive directions, and hence that the conditions of equilibrium are the same as those of Art. [16].

2°. Denoting the tensions of the portions AB and BC of the cord EABCF by S and Q, and the angles at A, B and C by s and p, q' and s', p^{IV} and q, as represented in the figure, and applying the principle of proportion [28], that the relations of the tensions P and P^{IV} will be given by the proportion

$$P \ : \ P^{\text{IV}} \ :: \ \sin p \times \sin s' \times \sin q \ : \ \sin s \times \sin q' \times \sin p^{\text{IV}}.$$

3°. That when the forces P', P'', P''', are parallel to each other [Fig. 36], and hence the sums $p + q'$, $s' + p^{\text{IV}}$, are each equal to 180°,

$$P \ : \ P^{\text{IV}} \ :: \ \sin q \ : \ \sin s.$$

4°. That when the cord EBF [Fig. 37], sustained

by the forces P and P^{iv} applied at E and F, is subjected to no other additional force than gravity,

$$P : P^{iv} : R :: \sin FMG : \sin EMG : \sin EMF;$$

R denoting the weight of the cord, and EM and FM being tangents to the cord at the points E and F, and MG a vertical line drawn through their point of meeting.

THE LEVER.

54. A lever is a bar or rod of any form whatever, capable of motion about a fixed axis or support called *the fulcrum*. In investigating the properties of the lever, we conceive it reduced to a material line.

Let the line ACBD [Fig. 38], represent a lever, and F its fulcrum; and suppose it to be acted upon by the forces P, P', etc. tending to turn it in one sense about the point F, and P'', P''', etc. tending to turn it in the opposite sense about this point, all the forces being supposed to act in the same plane. Also let the lines p, p', etc., p'', p''', etc. be drawn from F perpendicular to the directions of the forces. Then the conditions of equilibrium of the forces will be expressed by the equation [Art. 35],

$$Pp + P'p' + \text{etc.} = P''p'' + P'''p''' + \text{etc.}$$

In this equation, the forces P, P', etc. may be supposed to represent the powers applied to the lever, and P'', P''', etc. the resistances to be overcome. The weight of the lever may be regarded as a vertical force applied at its centre of gravity.

55. The case most frequently occuring in practice, is that in which only two forces act upon the lever. The preceding equation is then reduced to

$$Pp = P''p'',$$

and we have

$$P \ : \ P'' \ :: \ p'' \ : \ p.$$

Thus, in this case, *the power and the resistance are inversely as the perpendiculars drawn from the fulcrum to their directions.*

56. When the lever AB [Fig. 39] is straight, and the two forces act in parallel directions, we get from the similar triangles FAM, FBN,

$$p'' \ : \ p \ :: \ \mathrm{FB} \ : \ \mathrm{FA},$$

and hence we have

$$P \ : \ P'' \ :: \ \mathrm{FB} \ : \ \mathrm{FA};$$

that is, *the power and the resistance inversely as the distances of their points of application from the fulcrum.* These distances are called *the arms of the lever.*

57. The pressure upon the fulcrum is evidently equal to the resultant of all the forces which act upon the lever. When the lever is not retained by a fixed axis, but only rests upon a fixed support, it is essential to the equilibrium that the direction of the resultant should be perpendicular to the lever.

58. According to the relative positions of the power, the resistance and the fulcrum, levers have been divided into three kinds. A lever is said to be of the 1st kind, when the power and the resistance are applied on opposite sides of the fulcrum, as in

Fig. 40; of the 2d kind, when these forces are applied on the same side of the fulcrum, the resistance being the nearer to the fulcrum, as in Fig. 41; and of the 3d kind, when these forces are on the same side of F, and the power is the nearer to the fulcrum, as in Fig. 42.

THE INCLINED PLANE.

59. This machine consists essentially of a plane, inclined at any angle whatever to a horizontal plane. Conceive a body to be in equilibrium on an inclined plane: it is evident that the force P which prevents the body from sliding down the plane, and P' the gravity of the body, must have a resultant perpendicular to the plane, and meeting it within the limits of the base of the body. The plane of these forces will be vertical, and also perpendicular to the inclined plane. The section of the inclined plane and the body, by the plane of the forces, is represented in Fig. 43, in which AB is the section of the inclined plane, and MLN that of the body, and BC and AC are horizontal and vertical lines meeting each other at the point C; AB, BC and AC being the length, base, and height of the plane respectively. Let the line KE be the direction of the force P; KF, which we suppose to pass through the centre of gravity of the body, that of P'; and KG perpendicular to AB, that of the resultant R. Then denoting the angles as represented in the figure, we shall have

$$P \; : \; P' \; : \; R \; :: \; \sin p \; : \; \sin p' \; : \; \sin r;$$

or, since p is equal to i the inclination of the plane, and $\sin i = \frac{h}{l}$,

$$P : P' : R :: h : l \sin p' : l \sin r. \quad \ldots\ldots [29]$$

1°. When the direction of P is parallel to the inclined plane, $p' = 90°$, and we get from the above proportion,

$$P : P' :: h : l;$$

that is, *the power to the weight of the body, as the height of the plane to its length.*

2°. When the direction of P is parallel to the base of the plane, $p' = (90° - i)$, and we have

$$P : P' :: h : l \cos i$$
$$:: h : b;$$

that is, *the power to the weight, as the height of the plane to its base.*

We have regarded the plane as inclined with respect to the horizon, and supposed the force P' to be gravity; but the above results will obviously be true if we consider the plane as inclined with respect to any assumed plane, and substitute for gravity any force acting perpendicular to the latter plane.

THE PULLEY.

60. The pulley is a small grooved wheel, capable of motion about an axis, and having its circumference partly enveloped by a cord, to the extremities of which the forces are applied. The axis is supported by a frame called *the block;* and according as the block is fixed or capable of motion, the pulley is said to be fixed or movable.

61. *The fixed pulley.*

Let IGHK [Fig. 44] represent a fixed pulley, and EIKHF a cord enveloping the arc IKH of its circumference; and suppose the two forces P and Q to be applied at the points E and F, in the directions IE and HF tangent to the circumference at the points I and H. Produce EI and FH, and let the points of application of P and Q be transferred to A the point of meeting of these lines. Then since O is the only fixed point in the pulley, in order to an equilibrium, the direction of the resultant R of P and Q must pass through that point: hence it must bisect the angle EAF, and consequently the forces P and Q must be equal to each other. Let the resultant be represented by AD, and complete the parallelogram ABDC: then P and Q will be represented by the equal lines AB and AC respectively, and we shall have

$$P : R :: \mathrm{AB} : \mathrm{AD}.$$

But from the similar triangles ABD, IOH, we get

$$\mathrm{AB} : \mathrm{AD} :: \mathrm{IO} : \mathrm{IH};$$

consequently we have

$$P : R :: \mathrm{IO} : \mathrm{IH}.$$

Thus, in the fixed pulley, *each of the forces applied to the cord or rope is to their resultant, or the pressure upon the point of support, as the radius of the pulley is to the chord of the arc with which the rope is in contact.* The fixed pulley is employed, when it is desired to change the direction of a force without affecting its intensity.

62. *Movable pulley.*

In the movable pulley, one extremity of the cord is attached to a fixed point F [Fig. 45]; and a power P applied to the other extremity, holds in equilibrium a force R applied in a direction passing through the centre O. The resistance R is usually the weight of a body suspended from the centre. In place of the re-action of the fixed point F, we may substitute a force Q, and consider the machine as in equilibrium under the action of the forces P, Q and R, applied at points entirely free. The condition of equilibrium will obviously be, that the resultant of P and Q must be equal and contrary to R. Hence it may be readily inferred that P and Q are equal, and, as in the preceding case, that

$$P : R :: \mathrm{IO} : \mathrm{IH}.$$

Thus, in the movable pulley, *the power is to the resistance, as the radius of the pulley is to the chord of the arc in contact with the rope.*

1°. When the cords EI and FH are parallel, the chord IH becomes a diameter, and we have

$$P : R :: 1 : 2;$$

that is, *the resistance equal to twice the power.*

2°. When the arc IKH in contact with the cord is equal to 60°, we have

$$P = R;$$

and when this arc is less than 60°,

$$P > R.$$

L

63. *Systems of pulleys.*

1°. Let C, C′, C″, be a system of movable pulleys, connected with each other in the manner represented in Fig. 46, in which F, F′, F″, are fixed points, and the power P applied in the direction I″E holds in equilibrium the weight R suspended from C. Denoting the tensions of the cords IC′, I′C″ by P'' and P', we have

$$P'' : R :: \mathrm{IC} : \mathrm{IH},$$
$$P' : P'' :: \mathrm{I'C'} : \mathrm{I'H'},$$
$$P : P' :: \mathrm{I''C''} : \mathrm{I''H''};$$

and hence

$$P : R :: \mathrm{IC} \times \mathrm{I'C'} \times \mathrm{I''C''} : \mathrm{IH} \times \mathrm{I'H'} \times \mathrm{I''H''}.$$

That is, in this system of pulleys, *the power is to the resistance, as the product of the radii of the pulleys is to the product of the chords of the arcs in contact with the ropes.*

When the cords are parallel, as in Fig. 47, the above proportion is reduced to

$$P : R :: 1 : 2^3.$$

Hence, in a system of this kind, in which n movable pulleys are employed, we shall have

$$P : R :: 1 : 2^n.$$

By means of movable pulleys arranged in this manner, a great weight may be moved by a small force; but it will readily be perceived that the gain in power will be attended with a loss in respect to time.

2°. A combination more convenient than the preceding, is that in which several pulleys, both fixed and movable, are embraced by a single cord as represented in Fig. 48, in which the several parts x, y, z, etc. of the cord are supposed to be parallel to each other. In this arrangement, we may obviously consider the tensions of these portions of the cord as a system of equal and parallel forces acting in the same sense, of which the resultant is equal to the weight or resistance R. Thus in the case of three movable pulleys, in which the cord has six branches, we have

$$P : R :: 1 : 6;$$

and hence denoting the number of pulleys by n, we have generally

$$P : R :: 1 : 2n.$$

The method of determining the power necessary to put in equilibrium the weight of the several movable pulleys, is sufficiently obvious.

THE WHEEL AND AXLE.

64. This machine consists of a wheel AA′ [Fig. 49], and a cylinder or axle BB′, so adjusted as to have a common axis, and firmly connected with each other. The cylinder is supported at its extremities in such a manner as to admit of only a motion of rotation about the common axis. The power P and the resistance R are applied at points of the wheel and axle, respectively, in the direction of tangents to their circumferences. The mode of operation of the machine is indicated in the figure. The case of an

equilibrium between P and R in this machine is obviously comprehended in the more general case already considered in Art. 40. Referring then to this article, and denoting the radius of the wheel by p, and that of the axle by r, we get

$$Pp = Rr,$$

or
$$P : R :: r : p.$$

That is, in the equilibrium of the wheel and axle, *the power is to the resistance as the radius of the axle is to the radius of the wheel.*

When P and R act upon the machine by means of cords, we must suppose these forces applied to the axes of the cords, and increase the radii of both the wheel and axle by the radii of the cords respectively.

65. A combination of wheels and axles is sometimes used. One of these compound machines, in which three of the simpler machines are employed, is represented in figure 50. To find the relation in this case between the power P and the resistance P''', denote the tensions of the intermediate cords MN, M′N′, by P' and P''; the radii of the several wheels by p, p' and p''; and those of the corresponding axles by r, r', r'': then we shall have

$$P : P' :: r : p,$$
$$P' : P'' :: r' : p',$$
$$P'' : P''' :: r'' : p'';$$

and hence

$$P : P''' :: r \times r' \times r'' : p \times p' \times p'';$$

that is, *the power to the resistance, as the product of the radii of the axles to the product of the radii of the wheels.*

66. In these combinations, the connexion between the simple machines is frequently effected by means of teeth or cogs projecting from the several convex surfaces, as represented in figure 51. The relation between the power and the resistance is not altered by this modification of the mode of connexion.

THE SCREW.

67. This machine consists, 1st, of the *interior screw* (usually called simply the screw), a cylindrical solid, around whose convex surface passes a uniform band or *fillet*, oblique to the axis, and constantly inclined to it at the same angle; and, 2d, of the *exterior screw*, or *nut*, a hollow cylinder of the same diameter as the solid one, on the concave surface of which is a groove exactly adapted to the fillet of the interior screw. The mode of operation of this machine is indicated in figures 52 and 53, in which AB represents the interior screw, inserted in the nut CD; and OS, O′S′, two arms or levers to which the forces are respectively applied, according as it is desired to communicate motion to the nut or to the interior screw.

The investigation of the properties of the screw is best conducted by first considering the manner in which the fillet may be conceived to be generated.

Let ABDC [Fig. 54], be a cylinder, and BM a rectangle, of which the base DM is equal to the circumference of the base of the cylinder. Let the sides BD and NM be divided into the equal parts BF, FH, etc., NG, GI, etc.; and let the oblique lines FN, HG, etc. be drawn. Then if the rectangle be applied to the convex surface of the cylinder in such a manner that the line NM shall coincide with BD, the points N, G, I, etc. will coincide with the points B, F, H, etc., and the oblique lines FN, HG, etc. will form on the surface of the cylinder a continuous curve *ss'*. This curve is called *a helix;* and the constant interval NG, its *pitch.* If now we conceive a triangle, whose plane constantly passes through the axis of the cylinder, to revolve about that axis in such a manner that its base, never greater than NG, shall constantly be in contact with the cylinder, and have one of its extremities in the helix *ss'*, it is evident that each point of the revolving figure will describe a helix similar to *ss'*, and that the assemblage of helices thus described will form the fillet of a screw. The generating surface is usually a triangle, as we have above supposed it to be: it is sometimes a rectangle, and may be of any form whatever. The conditions of the problem being the same, whether we suppose the screw to be movable and the nut fixed, or the converse, we will adopt the latter hypothesis.

Let then the screw be supposed to be fixed, and the nut resting upon it to be subjected to the action of two forces: the one, the resistance R, acting directly upon it in the direction of the axis; the other, the power P, acting at S at right angles to the axis, and also to the lever OS. In the revolution of the nut, each of its points in contact with the screw describes, as we have seen, a helix, and may obviously be regarded as moving on an inclined plane whose height is equal to the pitch of the screw, and whose base is equal to the circumference of the circle having for its radius the distance of the point from the axis of the screw. Hence, considering a single point of contact M [Fig. 55], whose distance from the axis is OM, and denoting the forces which act upon it by p and r, both being supposed to act directly upon the point, the first parallel to the base of the plane, the second perpendicular to it, we shall have, in the case of an equilibrium [Art. 59, 2°],

$$p : r :: \mathrm{NG} : 2\pi \times \mathrm{OM}.$$

But if the power be applied at S instead of M, at the distance OS from the axis, we shall have, to determine the force P which, applied at S, will be equivalent to p applied at M, the proportion

$$P : p :: \mathrm{OM} : \mathrm{OS};$$

whence we get

$$P : p :: 2\pi \times \mathrm{OM} : 2\pi \times \mathrm{OS}.$$

Comparing this proportion with the first, we have

$$P : r :: \mathrm{NG} : 2\pi \times \mathrm{OS};$$

and hence

$$P = r \times \frac{\mathrm{NG}}{2\pi \times \mathrm{OS}}.$$

For the other points of contact M′, M″, etc., at which the resistances r', r'', etc. are put in equilibrium by the powers P', P'', etc., applied at the same distance from the axis as the power P, we have

$$P' = r' \times \frac{NG}{2\pi \times OS},$$

$$P'' = r'' \times \frac{NG}{2\pi \times OS},$$

etc.

Hence, denoting the sum of the powers P, P', etc. by $P_{,}$, and the sum of the resistances r, r', etc. by R, we have

$$P_{,} = R \times \frac{NG}{2\pi \times OS};$$

whence,

$$P_{,} \ : \ R \ :: \ NG \ : \ 2\pi \times OS.$$

That is, in the equilibrium of the screw, *the power is to the resistance, as the pitch of the screw, or the distance between the threads, is to the circumference of the circle described by the point of application of the power.*

THE WEDGE.

68. The wedge is a solid body of the shape of a triangular prism. The surface CDEF [Fig. 56], is called its *back;* ABED and ABFC, its *sides;* and AB the intersection of the sides, its *edge.* The use to which it is most commonly applied, is to separate the parts of a body, by introducing the edge AB into a small cleft, and applying an impulsive force to the back. Since the resistance, or the force which the parts of the body oppose to the separation, is always unknown, it would be useless to investigate the conditions of equilibrium between it and the power. We shall, therefore, seek merely the relation between

the power and its components perpendicular to the sides of the wedge.

Let MNO [Fig. 57] be a section of the wedge by a plane perpendicular to its edge. Let the power P, which we suppose to be perpendicular to NO, be represented by IK, and be resolved into the two components IR and IS perpendicular respectively to NM and OM. These components represent the effects of the power upon the sides of the wedge, and tend directly to separate the parts of the body. Denoting the power and its components by P, P' and P'' respectively, we have

$$P : P' : P'' :: \mathrm{IK} : \mathrm{IR} : \mathrm{IS}.$$

But from the similar triangles MNO and IKR, we have

$$\mathrm{IK} : \mathrm{IR} : \mathrm{IS} :: \mathrm{NO} : \mathrm{MN} : \mathrm{MO}:$$

hence

$$P : P' : P'' :: \mathrm{NO} : \mathrm{MN} : \mathrm{MO};$$

and multiplying the last three terms of this proportion by the line DE [Fig. 56] we get

$$P : P' : P'' :: \mathrm{NO} \times \mathrm{DE} : \mathrm{MN} \times \mathrm{DE} : \mathrm{MO} \times \mathrm{DE}.$$

The products composing the last three terms of this proportion represent the respective surfaces of the back and sides of the wedge. Consequently, in the wedge, *the power applied at right angles to the back, and the efforts exerted at the sides, are respectively proportional to the surfaces of the back and sides.*

GENERAL PRINCIPLE OF EQUILIBRIUM IN MACHINES.

69. By combining the simple machines above described, an endless variety of compound machines may be formed. In these compound machines, the ratio of the power to the resistance can be determined when the tensions of the cords which connect the various parts are known, as has been done in the case of the systems of pulleys of article 63, and that of wheels and axles of article 65. But in every case, however complex the machine, this ratio can also be determined by the following rule:

Let the equilibrium of the machine be supposed to suffer an infinitely small disturbance: the points of application of P and R, the power and the resistance, will describe infinitely small arcs. If the directions of P and R are tangent to these arcs, let the *arcs* be denoted by u and v respectively: if they are not, let the *projections of the arcs* upon the directions of P and R be denoted by these letters; then will the relation between P and R be expressed by the proportion

$$P : R :: v : u.$$

This rule is a particular case of a general principle of mechanics, called *the principle of virtual velocities.*

70. APPLICATIONS.

1°. *The lever.* 1st. Let AB [Fig. 58] represent the lever; and from F the fulcrum, let the perpendiculars p and p' be drawn to the directions of the two forces P and P'. Let M and N, the feet of the perpendiculars, be taken as the points of application of P and P'; and conceive an infinitely small motion to be communicated to the lever, causing these points to describe the infinitely small arcs Mm and Nn. The directions of P and P' being tangent to these arcs, denoting them by u and v, we shall have, by the rule,

$$P : P' :: v : u;$$

but $$v : u :: p' : p:$$

hence $$P : P' :: p' : p.$$

That is, the forces are inversely as the perpendiculars drawn from the fulcrum to their directions as found in article 55.

2d. Let the forces P and P' be supposed to be applied at the points A and B [Fig. 59] the extremities of the lever. In the case of motion, the directions of P and P' will not in general be tangent to the arcs AE and BG described by A and B; and in applying the rule, we must consider u and v as denoting the projections of AE and BG upon these directions.

To find the values of u and v, draw EC and GD perpendicular to the directions of P and P', and consider the infinitely small arcs AE and BG as straight lines perpendicular to the radii FA and FB: then we have the triangles MFA, CAE similar to each other, and also the triangles NFB, DBG; and hence we get

$$\text{FA} : \text{FM} :: \text{AE} : \text{AC or } u,$$

and $$\text{FB} : \text{FN} :: \text{BG} : \text{BD or } v;$$

and hence

$$u = \frac{\text{AE}}{\text{FA}} \times \text{FM}, \quad \text{and } v = \frac{\text{BG}}{\text{FB}} \times \text{FN}.$$

Applying the rule, we have

$$P : P' :: \frac{\text{BG}}{\text{FB}} \times \text{FN} : \frac{\text{AE}}{\text{FA}} \times \text{FM};$$

but $$\text{AE} : \text{BG} :: \text{FA} : \text{FB},$$

or $$\frac{\text{BG}}{\text{FB}} = \frac{\text{AE}}{\text{FA}}:$$

consequently

$$P : P' :: \text{FN} : \text{FM},$$

or $$P : P' :: p' : p.$$

2°. *Wheel and axle.* In the wheel and axle, the directions of the forces P and R [Fig. 48] are tangent to the arcs described by their points of application: hence, denoting the arcs by u and v respectively, we have, by the rule,

$$P : R :: v : u;$$

but $$v : u :: r : p:$$

hence $$P : R :: r : p.$$

3°. *The screw.* In the screw, the direction ST [Fig. 52] of the power is not tangent to the arc of the helix described by S its point of application. Hence, in the proportion

$$P : R :: v : u,$$

we must regard u as denoting the projection upon ST of an infinitely small arc described by the point S; v being the corresponding space described by any point of the nut, in the direction of the axis of the screw. Conceive a plane to pass through OS perpendicular to the axis, and let the helix described by the point S be projected upon this plane; the projection will be the circumference of the circle of which OS is the radius. Now since ST is tangent to the circumference of the circle, the projection of the infinitely small arc of the helix upon this line will be equal to its projection upon the circumference, and the one may be taken for the other. Considering then u as an arc of the circle, it is evident from the nature of the helix, that v is to u, as the pitch NG [Fig. 55] of the screw is to the circumference of the circle of which OS [Fig. 52] is the radius, or that

$$v : u :: \mathrm{NG} : 2\pi \times \mathrm{OS};$$

whence we get

$$P : R :: \mathrm{NG} : 2\pi \times \mathrm{OS}.$$

4°. *Systems of pulleys.* We will consider the system of pulleys represented in figure 48. Denoting the spaces described by the points of application of the forces P and R by u and v respectively, we have, by the rule,

$$P : R :: v : u.$$

But when, by the action of P, the weight R is elevated through the space m, each of the six branches of the cord embracing the movable pulleys is shortened by the same quantity; and hence the point of application of the power must descend through the space $6m$. Hence we have

$$v : u :: 1 : 6,$$

and consequently

$$P : R :: 1 : 6.$$

FRICTION.

71. A perfectly smooth body, placed on an inclined plane also perfectly smooth, would move, if abandoned to the action of gravity, however slight the inclination of the plane; but in practice this motion never takes place, till the angle of inclination reaches a certain magnitude, greater or less according to the circumstances of the case. The reason of this is, that the surfaces of even the most highly polished bodies are only comparatively smooth, and consequently the sliding of one surface upon another is always attended with a certain resistance. This resistance is called *friction.*

Let the body MN [Fig. 60] be placed on a plane AB, and let the angle of inclination of the plane be gradually increased till it reaches the magnitude i, at which the body just begins to move. In this position of the plane, let P the weight of the body applied at its centre of gravity C, and represented by CF, be resolved into the two components

$$CG = P \cos i, \quad \text{and } CE = P \sin i,$$

the one perpendicular to the plane, the other parallel to it. The first will obviously measure the pressure of the body upon the plane; the second, its friction. If now while the surface in contact with the plane remains the same, the weight P, and hence the pressure $P \cos i$, be made to vary, the angle of inclination at which the body begins to move will be found to be unaffected, retaining constantly its first value i: whence we infer,

1°. *That the friction is directly proportional to the pressure.*

Denoting the friction by F, the pressure by P', and the ratio of the two by f, we have

$$f = \frac{F}{P'} = \text{tang}\, i,$$

and

$$F = P' \times \text{tang}\, i.$$

The angle i is called *the angle of friction,* and the constant f *the coefficient of friction.* The latter expresses the friction for the unit of pressure, and is taken as the measure of friction.

If the body MN be a polyhedron whose faces are unequal in extent, but equally polished, the angle i at which it will begin to move will be found to be the same, on whichever face it may rest upon the plane: whence it appears,

2°. *That the friction is independent of the extent of the surface in contact.*

It is also found,

3°. *That the friction is independent of the velocity;* that is, that the friction is the same, whatever the velocity with which the one surface moves over the other.

PART SECOND.

DYNAMICS.

OF THE RECTILINEAR MOTION OF A MATERIAL POINT.

I. *Of uniform rectilinear motion.*

1. UNIFORM rectilinear motion is that in which a material point, moving in a right line, passes over equal spaces in equal times. It is the simplest kind of motion, and takes place whenever a body is acted upon by an impulsive force, and then abandoned to itself.

The velocity of the point is the space which it describes in the interval of time arbitrarily chosen as the unit. It evidently expresses the rate at which the point moves.

If the velocity be denoted by v, then

The space described at the end of the			1st	unit of time,	is	v,
"	"	"	2d	"	"	$2v$,
"	"	"	3d	"	"	$3v$,
"	"	"	"	....		
"	"	"	tth	"	"	tv;

and denoting the whole space by s, we have

$$s = vt. \qquad [1]$$

§ 1. From the preceding equation, we get

$$v = \frac{s}{t};$$

from which it appears, that in uniform motion, the velocity is the ratio of the space described to the time employed in describing it.

§ 2. If we denote by s' and s'' the spaces passed over in the times t' and t'' by two points moving uniformly with the velocities v' and v'', we have

$$s' = v't',$$

$$s'' = v''t'';$$

and hence $\quad s' \;:\; s'' \;::\; v't' \;:\; v''t'';$

that is, the spaces described are as the products of the times by the velocities.

When the times are equal, we have

$$s' \;:\; s'' \;::\; v' \;:\; v'',$$

or the spaces as the velocities.

When the velocities are equal, we have

$$s' \;:\; s'' \;::\; t' \;:\; t'',$$

or the spaces as the times.

When the spaces are equal, we have

$$t' \;:\; t'' \;::\; v'' \;:\; v',$$

or the times inversely as the spaces.

2. A more general form may be given to equation [1]. Thus [Fig. 1] suppose the material point to be moving on the line AB from left to right, with a velocity v, and denote by s its distance at any instant

from the point O arbitrarily assumed on AB, and let the time t be reckoned from the instant at which the point is at O′; then when the point is at D to the right of O′, we have

$$OD = OO' + O'D,$$

or, putting, $OO' = b,$

$$s = vt + b. \quad\ldots\ldots\ldots\ldots\ldots\ldots [2]$$

In this equation, the variables s and t may be either positive or negative. The positive values of t refer to times posterior to the instant at which the point is at O′; the negative values, to times anterior to the same instant. The positive values of s must be reckoned from O to the right; the negative values, from O to the left.

In this general form, the equation will enable us to determine, at any instant whatever, the position of the material point on the indefinite straight line AB.

If we suppose another material point to move in the line AB with a velocity v', and to be at O″ at the instant at which the first point is at O′, its motion will be determined by the equation

$$s' = v't + b'; \quad\ldots\ldots\ldots\ldots\ldots\ldots [3]$$

s' denoting its variable distance from O, and b' the distance OO″.

By means of equations [2] and [3], any problem may be solved, which depends upon the relative motions of the two points. Thus, to determine when the two points will meet each other, in which case

$$s = s',$$

we have $$vt + b = v't' + b',$$

and hence get $$t = \frac{b' - b}{v - v'}.$$

II. *Of motion uniformly varied.*

3. A force which acts without intermission, and with a constant intensity, is called *a constant accelerating force.* The motion of a material point, subjected to the action of a constant accelerating force, is called *a uniformly varied motion.*

Let a material point be supposed to be acted upon by a constant accelerating force; then if at any instant the accelerating force cease to act, the motion will evidently become uniform, and the point will move with the velocity which it had at that instant. Hence in motion uniformly varied, the velocity at any instant is the space which the point would describe in any succeeding unit of time, should the accelerating force at that instant cease to act. The velocity evidently depends upon the intensity of the force, and the time during which it has been acting.

Since a constant accelerating force acts at every instant with the same intensity, it must generate equal velocities in equal times. We assume as the measure of a constant accelerating force, the velocity which it generates in the unit of time.

Let us now suppose a material point to move from a state of rest, under the action of a constant accelerating force, of which the intensity is denoted by g; and let us seek the velocity v, and s the space described, at the end of the time t.*

To facilitate the investigation, conceive the time divided into an infinite number of infinitely small equal intervals, or *instants*; and suppose the force to act upon the point at the commencement of each instant. Then during each instant the motion will be uniform, and the variable motion will be resolved into a series of uniform motions.

Denote by n the number of instants in a single unit of time, and by k the number of instants in the whole period t; then

$$k = nt.$$

Also let i equal the space which the point describes during an instant, in virtue of the constant velocity which the force communicates to it at the beginning of each instant; then the spaces described by the point during the successive instants of the time t, will be

$$i, \quad 2i, \quad 3i, \quad ni, \quad ki. \qquad\qquad [4]$$

If at the end of the first second the accelerating force should cease to act, the point, having during the nth instant described the space ni, would, during the following second, describe the space $n.ni = n^2i$;

* The time t is given in terms of the unit of time; that is, if the second be taken as the unit, t denotes a certain number of seconds.

and this being the velocity communicated during the preceding second, or the measure of the accelerating force, we shall have

$$g = n^2 i.$$

If at the end of the time t we suppose the accelerating force to cease acting, the point, which in the kth instant has described the space ki, will, in the following second, describe the space $n \times ki = nki$; and this will be the velocity acquired at the end of the time t. Denoting this by v, we shall have

$$v = nki;$$

but

$$k = nt;$$

hence

$$v = n^2 it$$

$$= gt. \qquad [5]$$

To find the space s, we have only to determine the sum of the series [4]: we thus have

$$s = (i + ki)\frac{k}{2}$$

$$= (1 + k)\frac{ik}{2};$$

but k being infinite, $(1 + k)$ becomes k, and we have

$$s = \frac{ik^2}{2} = \frac{n^2 it^2}{2} = \frac{gt^2}{2}. \qquad [6]$$

4. We have supposed the material point to be at rest when the accelerating force begins to act upon it: if we suppose it to be in motion, and to have al-

ready described a space b with a constant velocity a, we shall have the more general equations

$$v = a + gt, \quad \dots\dots\dots\dots \quad [7]$$

$$s = b + at + \tfrac{1}{2}gt^2. \quad \dots\dots\dots\dots \quad [8]$$

If the accelerating force act in the direction opposite to the primitive impulse, g must be affected with the negative sign. The motion in this case is said to be *uniformly retarded.*

If we suppose $g = o$, the equations are reduced to those of uniform motion.

5. If a material point, moving from a state of rest under the action of a constant accelerating force g, describe the spaces s and s' in the times t and t', and acquire the velocities v and v', equations [5] and [6] give

$$v = gt, \qquad v' = gt';$$

$$s = \tfrac{1}{2}gt^2, \quad s' = \tfrac{1}{2}gt'^2;$$

and hence we have the proportions

$$s : s' :: t^2 : t'^2,$$

$$v : v' :: t : t',$$

$$v : v' :: \sqrt{s} : \sqrt{s'};$$

that is, in motion uniformly accelerated, the spaces described are as the squares of the times, and the velocities acquired are as the times, or as the square roots of the spaces.

6. If in the equation $s = \frac{1}{2}gt^2$, we make $t = 1$, we get

$$s = \tfrac{1}{2}g, \text{ or } g = 2s;$$

that is, the velocity acquired in the unit of time is equal to twice the space described during that time; and hence, as the unit of time is arbitrary, it follows that a constant accelerating force communicates to a material point, in any time whatever, a velocity equal to twice the space which it causes the point to describe in the same time.

7. It can be shown by direct experiment, that bodies, near the surface of the earth, fall with a uniformly accelerated motion. Terrestrial gravity may therefore be considered a constant accelerating force; and hence equations [7] and [8] may be employed to determine the circumstances of the motion of falling bodies. To find the numerical value of g when it represents the intensity of gravity, we have recourse to an indirect process, which will be explained hereafter. It has thus been found, that in the latitude of the city of New-York, *the second being assumed as the unit of time,*

$$g = 32{,}1598 \text{ feet, or nearly } 32\tfrac{1}{6} \text{ feet.}$$

8. If from the equations

$$s = \tfrac{1}{2}gt^2 \text{ and } v = gt,$$

we eliminate t, we find

$$v = \sqrt{2gs}, \qquad [9]$$

an equation which gives the velocity acquired in falling through a given height, or, as it is usually expressed, the velocity due to a given height.

To determine the time in which a body will fall through a given height, we have the equation

$$t = \sqrt{\frac{2s}{g}}. \quad\dots\dots\dots\dots \text{[10]}$$

9. To determine the circumstances of the motion of a body projected vertically upwards: in equations [7] and [8], we make $b = 0$, and affect g with the negative sign; we thus get

$$v = a - gt, \quad\dots\dots\dots\dots \text{[a]}$$

$$s = at - \tfrac{1}{2}gt^2, \quad\dots\dots\dots\dots \text{[b]}$$

in which a denotes the velocity of projection.

To find the time during which the body is ascending: in equation [a], we make $v = 0$; we thus get

$$t = \frac{a}{g}.$$

To find the greatest elevation of the body, we substitute this value of t in equation [b]: we thus get

$$s = \frac{a^2}{2g}.$$

The body having attained its greatest elevation, to find the velocity which it will acquire during its descent: in the equation $v = \sqrt{2gs}$, we substitute for s the expression $\frac{a^2}{2g}$; we thus get

$$v = a.$$

From this last result, it appears that the velocity acquired during the fall is equal to the velocity of projection.

10. A force acting without intermission, and constantly varying in intensity during the time of its action, according to some law, is called *a variable accelerating force.*

The velocity of a point moving under the action of a variable accelerating force, is measured in the same manner as in motion uniformly varied.

The measure of the intensity of a variable accelerating force, at any instant, is the velocity which it would generate, should it act during the unit of time with the intensity which it has at that instant. Thus a point being in motion under the action of a variable accelerating force, to determine the measure of the force at the end of the time t, conceive the force at that instant to cease varying, and to act during the succeeding second with the intensity which it has at that instant; the velocity acquired by the point during the second is the measure of the force. Let this velocity be denoted by φ; then the velocity acquired during the infinitely small interval of time t', immediately succeeding t, is evidently $\varphi t'$; and denoting this velocity, which is also infinitely small, by v', we have $\varphi t' = v'$, and hence

$$\varphi = \frac{v'}{t'}.$$

For the case of a constant accelerating force, we have

$$g = \frac{v}{t}.$$

Hence the measure of an accelerating force is the

same, whether it be constant or variable; only in the latter case the time and velocity, of which the ratio is taken, are infinitely small.

Experiments made near the surface of the earth indicate, as already remarked, no variation in the intensity of gravity at different points of the same vertical. A more extended induction, however, shows that gravity is really a variable force. The general law is, as will be seen in a subsequent article, that the intensity of gravity depends upon the distance of the point at which it acts, from the centre of the earth; the intensities at any two points of the same vertical being inversely as the squares of the distances. It can be shown, by a very simple calculation, that according to this law, the motion of a falling body near the surface of the earth should not differ sensibly from a uniformly accelerated motion.

OF THE MOTION OF BODIES UPON INCLINED PLANES.

11. The motion of a body placed on an inclined plane, and abandoned to the action of gravity, may evidently be reduced to that of a material point under the same circumstances.*

To consider the motion of a material point on an inclined plane, conceive the inclined plane to be

*It may be proper to remark, that throughout the following pages the body whose motion is the subject of investigation is considered to be under the influence of the *enumerated* forces alone. Thus, in the present case, it is supposed to be acted upon by gravity only, abstraction being made of friction and the resistance of the medium in which the motion takes place.

intersected at right angles by a vertical plane, and suppose the section to be represented by AB [Fig. 2.]; and from A and B let the lines AC and BC be drawn, vertical and horizontal respectively. Denote the angle at B by i, and the height and length of the plane by h and l respectively. A material point, placed on the plane at A, will evidently describe the line AB.

Suppose the point to be at M; and let g, the intensity of gravity, be represented by the vertical MP. Let MP be resolved into the two components MR and MQ, the one in the line AB, the other perpendicular to it; the latter will be destroyed by the reaction of the plane, and the former will cause the point to describe the line AB.

The angle MPR being equal to the angle at B, we have

$$MR = g \sin i.$$

Thus the force which urges the material point down the inclined plane is of the same nature as gravity, differing from it only in intensity. If, therefore, in the equations of uniformly varied motion,

$$v = gt, \quad s = \tfrac{1}{2}gt^2 \text{ and } v = \sqrt{2gs},$$

we substitute $g \sin i$ in place of g, we shall have, to determine the circumstances of the motion of the point, the equations

$$v = gt \sin i, \qquad [11]$$

$$s = \tfrac{1}{2}gt^2 \sin i, \qquad [12]$$

$$v = \sqrt{2gs \sin i}. \qquad [13]$$

If the point be made to ascend the plane by an impulse in the direction BA, the motion will be determined by the equations

$$v = a - gt \sin i,$$

$$s = at - \tfrac{1}{2}gt^2 \sin i,$$

a denoting the velocity due to the impulse.

12. To determine the velocity acquired by the material point in describing the line AB, we have the equation

$$v = \sqrt{2gs \sin i}$$

$$= \sqrt{2gl \sin i}$$

$$= \sqrt{2gh}.$$

But $\sqrt{2gh}$ is the velocity which the point would acquire in falling through the height h or AC: hence it appears that a material point acquires the same velocity in descending the length of an inclined plane, that it would acquire in falling freely through the height of the plane; and, consequently, that if several material points, setting out from the same point A [Fig. 3], and moving on different inclined planes, describe the lines AB, AB′, AB″, on arriving at the points B, B′, B″, situated in the same horizontal plane, they will all have acquired the same velocity.

13. To find the relations of the times t and t' employed in describing the lengths l and l' of two inclined planes of which the heights are h and h', we get from equation [12]

$$t^2 = \frac{s}{\frac{1}{2}g \cdot \sin i}$$

$$= \frac{l}{\frac{1}{2}g} \times \frac{l}{h} = \frac{l^2}{\frac{1}{2}gh},$$

and hence $$t = \frac{l}{\sqrt{\frac{1}{2}g} \cdot \sqrt{h}}.$$

Hence, for the second plane, we have

$$t' = \frac{l'}{\sqrt{\frac{1}{2}g} \cdot \sqrt{h'}};$$

and consequently we have

$$t : t' :: \frac{l}{\sqrt{h}} : \frac{l'}{\sqrt{h'}};$$

that is, the times employed by two material points in describing two different inclined planes, are as the lengths of the planes divided by the square roots of the heights. Hence when the heights of the two planes are equal, the times are simply as the lengths.

14. Let AB [Fig. 4] represent the line described by a material point in descending an inclined plane; and from D any point whatever of the altitude AC, draw DE perpendicular to AB. Then denoting the angle at B by i, and by t the time in which a material point will describe the line AE, we have [equa. 12]

$$\text{AE} = \tfrac{1}{2}gt^2 \sin i;$$

but $$\text{AE} = \text{AD} \cdot \sin i;$$

hence $$\tfrac{1}{2}gt^2 \sin i = \text{AD} \cdot \sin i,$$

and $$t = \sqrt{\frac{\text{AD}}{\frac{1}{2}g}}.$$

Again, denoting by t' the time in which a material point will describe the line ED, we shall find by a similar operation,

$$t' = \sqrt{\frac{\text{AD}}{\frac{1}{2}g}}.$$

But $\sqrt{\frac{\text{AD}}{\frac{1}{2}g}}$ is the expression of the time [equa. 10] in which a material point, moving freely, will descend from A to D; and the point E is in the circumference of the circle described on AD as a diameter: hence a material point, moving in the plane of a vertical circle, will describe any chord drawn from either extremity of the vertical diameter, in the same time that it will describe the diameter itself.

OF THE MOTION OF A MATERIAL POINT ON A GIVEN CURVE.

15. From any point M [Fig. 5] of the circumference of a circle ABD, let the straight line MP be drawn perpendicular to the diameter AB; then

$$\text{AP} : \text{PM} :: \text{PM} : \text{PB}.$$

If we suppose the arc BM to be infinitely small, we shall have PM infinitely small with respect to AP, and hence PB infinitely small with respect to PM; that is, PB will be an infinitely small quantity of the second order. But PB is the versed sine of the arc BM; hence the versed sine of an infinitely small arc is an infinitely small quantity of the second order.

16. Let AB, BC [Fig. 6] be two contiguous sides of the perimeter of a polygon; and let a material

point, which is constrained to describe this perimeter, be supposed to have arrived at B with a velocity v. Let v be represented by BD a portion of AB produced, and be resolved into the two velocities BN, BM, the one in the direction of BC, the other perpendicular to it: the latter is destroyed by the reaction of the side BC; the former is the velocity with which the point describes this side.

The velocity lost by the point in passing from the side AB to BC is evidently equal to BD — BN. But denoting the angle NBD by u, we have

$$\mathrm{BN} = v \cos u;$$

hence we have

$$\begin{aligned} \text{the velocity lost} &= v - v \cos u \\ &= v\,(1 - \cos u) \\ &= v \,.\, \text{vers sin} u. \end{aligned}$$

If now we suppose the given polygon to become a a polygon of an infinite number of infinitely small sides, or a curve, the angle u, which any side makes with the adjacent side produced, will become infinitely small; and hence (Art. 15) the velocity lost in passing from the one side to the other will be an infinitely small quantity of the second order. When, therefore, a material point is constrained to describe a curve, under the action of either impulsive or accelerating forces, it retains all the velocity which is communicated to it in a direction tangent to the curve; for since the velocity lost at each angle of the polygon is an infinitely small quantity of the second order, the whole velocity lost in passing over a curve of finite length can only be the sum of an infinite number of infinitely small quantities of the second order, that is, an infinitely small quantity of the first order.

17. Let ABCD, etc. [Fig. 7] be a vertical curve, or polygon of an infinite number of infinitely small sides AB, BC, CD, etc.; and let the sides be produced to meet the horizontal line KH in A, E, H, etc. Then a material point starting from A, and constrained to describe the perimeter ABCD, etc., under the action of gravity, will have, when it arrives at the point B, the same velocity as if it had described the line EB [Art. 12]; and as by the preceding article it loses no velocity in passing from AB to BC, when it arrives at C, it will have the same velocity as if it had described the line EC. In the same way it may be shown that at D it will have the same velocity as if it had described the line HD, or the vertical GD. Hence, generally, a material point which descends under the action of gravity, along a vertical curve, has, at any point whatever, the same velocity as if it had fallen freely from a height equal to that of the arc described. It is also evident that this velocity is independent of the form of the curve; so that several material points, setting out from the same point O [Fig. 8], and describing in the descent different curves OM, OM′, OM″, etc., will, on arriving at the same horizontal plane MM″, have the same velocity.

18. Let AMA′ [Fig. 9] be a curve, symmetrical with respect to the vertical MG, in which the points A and A′ are in the same horizontal line, and MT is the horizontal tangent; and suppose a material point, placed on the curve at A, to be abandoned to the action of gravity. It will acquire, in descending to the point M, a velocity due to the height GM, and, in virtue of this velocity, will rise in the branch MA′. But the velocity with which it will describe the arc MA′ will be constantly diminished by the action of gravity, and evidently in such a manner that, at any point, as m', its velocity will be the same that it was at m, m and m' being in the same horizontal line: hence at A′ its velocity will be reduced to zero. From A′ the point will descend to M, and acquire as before the velocity due to the height GM; and this velocity will just serve to carry it back to the point A from which it set out, and thus it will continue to oscillate for an indefinite time between A and A′. Since any element of the curve is described with the same velocity, whether the point is ascending or descending, it is clear that the time of the ascent in either of the branches is equal to the time of the descent in the same branch: it is also evident that the two branches are described in equal times. The point will therefore occupy the same time in going from A to A′, as in returning from A′ to A; and thus all the oscillations will be made in equal times. Oscillations which are thus made in equal times, are said to be *isochronous*.

OF THE SIMPLE PENDULUM.

19. A pendulum is an apparatus consisting of a solid body attached to one extremity of a rod, through the other extremity of which passes a horizontal axis, about which the whole system is capable of oscillating.

When the vertical, drawn through the centre of gravity of the system, meets the axis of rotation, the pendulum is at rest; but if it be removed from this position, and abandoned to the action of gravity, it makes a series of oscillations, which may be shown to be isochronous, and consequently may be employed to measure time. Such a pendulum is called *a compound pendulum*. To acquire a knowledge of its properties, we first investigate those of a purely ideal pendulum, called *the simple pendulum*. In this pendulum, the solid body of the compound pendulum is supposed to be reduced to a heavy material point, and the rod to a line inextensible and inflexible, and without gravity.

Let CB [Fig. 10] be a simple pendulum, suspended at C; and let it be withdrawn from the vertical position CK, and made to assume the position CB. Let the intensity of gravity, represented by BN, be resolved into the two components BQ and BP, the one in the direction of CB, the other perpendicular to it. Of these two components, the latter alone communicates motion to the pendulum, the former expending itself in producing a pressure upon the point C. The case is then precisely similar to that of a heavy material point compelled to describe a curve, the reaction of the fixed point taking the place of the resistance of the curve.

Suppose the pendulum, or material point, to have already descended from B to M [Fig. 11], and to have acquired in the descent a velocity u. Draw the horizontal line BD, and the vertical diameter HK. Also from the extremities of the arc MM′, supposed to be infinitely small, draw MP, M′P′ perpendicular to HK; and on AK as a diameter, describe the circumference ANO. Draw also M′O′ perpendicular to MP, and join C and M′.

Let AP′ $= x$, M′P′ $= y$, PP′ $= s$, AK $= b$, M′C $= l$; and denote the time in which the pendulum describes the arc MM′ by t'.

On account of the smallness of the arc MM′, we may suppose it to be described with a constant velocity u: hence we immediately have

$$t' = \frac{\text{MM}'}{u}.$$

But the triangles M′CP′, MM′O′, having their sides mutually perpendicular, are similar, and give

$$\text{M}'\text{P}' : \text{M}'\text{C} :: \text{M}'\text{O}' : \text{MM}';$$

and hence $$\text{MM}' = \frac{\text{M}'\text{O}' \times \text{M}'\text{C}}{\text{M}'\text{P}'}$$

$$= \frac{\text{PP}' \times \text{M}'\text{C}}{\text{M}'\text{P}'} = s \cdot \frac{l}{y}; \quad \text{[c]}$$

and [Art. 17] $$u = \sqrt{2gx},$$

whence $$t' = \frac{l}{y} \cdot \frac{s}{\sqrt{2gx}}.$$

Now $$(M'P')^2 = P'K \times P'H,$$

or $$y = \sqrt{(b-x) \times (2l - (b-x))};$$

and if we suppose the oscillations of the pendulum to be made in very small arcs, $(b-x)$ may be neglected in comparison with $2l$, and we shall have

$$y = \sqrt{(b-x)\, 2l}.$$

Substituting this value of y in the expression for t', we get

$$t' = \frac{ls}{\sqrt{2gx} \cdot \sqrt{2l\,(b-x)}}$$

$$= \frac{\sqrt{l} \cdot \frac{1}{2}s}{\sqrt{g} \cdot \sqrt{x\,(b-x)}}$$

$$= \frac{\sqrt{l}}{b\sqrt{g}} \times \frac{\frac{1}{2}bs}{\sqrt{x\,(b-x)}}.$$

But, applying the result contained in equation [c] to the circle ANKO, we get

$$NN' = \frac{PP' \times \frac{1}{2}AK}{N'P'} = \frac{PP' \times \frac{1}{2}AK}{\sqrt{AP' \times P'K}} = \frac{\frac{1}{2}bs}{\sqrt{x\,(b-x)}},$$

and hence we have $t' = \frac{\sqrt{l}}{\sqrt{g}} \times \frac{NN'}{b}$.

Now for the time of describing each of the indefinitely small arcs composing the finite arc BMK, a similar expression may be found; thus, for t'' the time of describing the indefinitely small arc M′M″, we should get

$$t'' = \frac{\sqrt{l}}{\sqrt{g}} \times \frac{N'N''}{b}.$$

Hence if we denote the time of describing the whole arc BKD by T, we shall have

$$\tfrac{1}{2}\mathrm{T} = \frac{\sqrt{l}}{\sqrt{g}} \times \frac{\text{arc ANK}}{b},$$

and
$$\mathrm{T} = \frac{\sqrt{l}}{\sqrt{g}} \times \frac{2\,\text{arc ANK}}{b}$$

$$= \pi \,.\, \frac{\sqrt{l}}{\sqrt{g}}, \qquad [14]$$

π being the ratio of the circumference of a circle to its diameter.

From this expression, it appears that when a pendulum oscillates in very small arcs, the time of an oscillation is independent of the height AK which determines the extent of the arc described; and hence that oscillations of small extent will be isochronous, though the amplitudes should vary.

20. Let l and l' be the lengths of two pendulums which oscillate in the times T and T′, under the action of gravity of different intensities denoted respectively by g and g'; then we shall have

$$\mathrm{T} = \pi\sqrt{\frac{l}{g}}, \text{ and } \mathrm{T}' = \pi\sqrt{\frac{l'}{g'}},$$

and hence $\mathrm{T} : \mathrm{T}' :: \sqrt{\frac{l}{g}} : \sqrt{\frac{l'}{g'}}$; .... [d]

that is, the times of oscillation are directly as the square roots of the lengths of the pendulums, and inversely as the square roots of the intensities of gravity.

§ 1. If the intensities of gravity are the same, we have

$$T : T' :: \sqrt{l} : \sqrt{l'};$$

and if n and n' denote the number of oscillations made by the two pendulums in a given time k, then

$$T = \frac{k}{n}, \text{ and } T' = \frac{k}{n'},$$

and
$$\frac{k}{n} : \frac{k}{n'} :: \sqrt{l} : \sqrt{l'},$$

or
$$n'^2 : n^2 :: l : l',$$

and
$$l = \frac{l' \cdot n'^2}{n^2}.$$

By means of this equation, we can calculate for any place the length of the pendulum which will make a given number of oscillations in a determinate time, when we know the number of oscillations which a pendulum of given length makes at the same place in the same time. Any small error that may be made in determining the time k, may be rendered insensible by taking n the number of oscillations sufficiently large. It is thus that the length of the seconds pendulum in the latitude of the city of New-York, that is, the pendulum which in that latitude makes 86400 oscillations in a mean solar day, in vacuo, has been found to be

39,in.10168, or 3,ft.25847.

§ 2. The measure of the intensity of gravity (already given Art. 7), may now be found. For this purpose, we employ the equation

$$T = \pi \sqrt{\frac{l}{g}}.$$

From it we get $g = \frac{\pi^2 \, . \, l}{T^2}$;

and making $T = 1''$, $\pi = 3{,}1415926$, and $l = 39{,}^{\text{in.}}10168$,

we find $g = 385{,}^{\text{in.}}9183 = 32{,}^{\text{ft.}}1598$.

The value of l, and consequently that of g, has been found to vary with the latitude of the place.

§ 3. If we suppose the lengths of the two pendulums to be equal, proportion [d] becomes

$$T : T' :: \sqrt{g'} : \sqrt{g};$$

and denoting by n and n' the number of oscillations made by the pendulums in any given time, we have

$$n' : n :: \sqrt{g'} : \sqrt{g},$$

or $g : g' :: n^2 : n'^2$; .... [e]

that is, the intensities of gravity at any two places are to each other as the squares of the number of oscillations made at the places in any given time, either by the same pendulum, or by two pendulums of equal lengths. Hence by causing the same pendulum to oscillate at places in different latitudes, the relative intensities of gravity at these places can be obtained. It has thus been found that the intensity of gravity increases as we proceed from the equator towards the poles. The relation between the ellipticity of the earth, and the intensity of gravity at different points of its surface, are such that the one can be found by means of the other: experiments with the pendulum thus furnish a means of determining the figure of the earth.

The principle expressed in proportion [e], is employed in determining the law of the intensities of the electrical and magnetic forces.

OF CENTRAL FORCES.

21. Let a material point be supposed to be in motion, in virtue of a primitive impulse, and an accelerating force which constantly solicits it towards a fixed point. Let the accelerating force be supposed to act at infinitely small equal intervals, or instants; communicating to the point, at the commencement of each instant, an infinitely small velocity. Let C [Fig. 12] be the fixed point through which the direction of the accelerating force constantly passes; and suppose the material point to be moving in the line MN, with a velocity which would cause it to describe the infinitely small space M′N in an instant. When the point arrives at M′, let the accelerating force be supposed to communicate to it a velocity which, were it at rest, would cause it to describe the space M′G in an instant; then the point will describe, during the instant, the diagonal M′M″ constructed on M′N, M′G. Arrived at M″, the point, if left to itself, would move in M′M″ produced, and in the following instant describe the line M″N′ equal to M′M″; but at M″, the accelerating force again acts; and if we

represent the space which it alone would cause the point to describe in an instant by M″G′, we shall have M″M‴ for the space actually described during the instant. It may thus be shown, that as long as the accelerating force continues to act, the point will move on the perimeter of a polygon, the sides of which, being infinitely small and all in the same plane, form a plane curve. The plane of the curve is evidently that which contains at the same time the fixed point, and the direction of the primitive impulse.

The velocity of the point, at any instant, is the space which it would describe in the direction of the element of the curve in which it is then moving, should the accelerating force at that instant cease to act.

The line drawn from the fixed point C to the position of the material point at any instant, is called *the radius vector.*

22. The areas described by the radius vector, in any two consecutive instants, are equal. For the triangles M′CM″, M″CN′ having equal bases and a common vertex C, are equal; and so also are the triangles M″CN′ and M″CM‴, which have the same base M″C, and their vertices situated in the same straight line parallel to the base. Hence the triangles M′CM″, M″CM‴, that is, the spaces described by the radius vector in two consecutive instants, are equal. But the areas in any two consecutive instants being equal, the areas described in any two equal intervals of

time must also be equal, since each interval contains the same number of instants; and, hence, generally, the areas described in any two intervals of time are proportional to the intervals. Thus when a material point describes a curve, in virtue of a primitive impulse, and an accelerating force which constantly solicits it towards a fixed point, *the areas described by the radius vector are proportional to the times employed in describing them.*

Conversely, when a material point, which describes about a fixed point a plane curve, moves so that the radius vector describes areas proportional to the times, *the direction of the accelerating force constantly passes through the fixed point.*

For, employing the preceding construction, the areas being proportional to the times, and hence the triangles described by the radius vector in any two consecutive instants being equal, we have the triangle

$$CM''M''' = CM'M'';$$

but we also have $CM'M'' = CM''N'$;

therefore $CM''M''' = CM''N'$,

and hence the line $N'M'''$ which joins the vertices of these triangles must be parallel to the common base CM''. But $N'M'''$ must be parallel to the accelerating force which acts at M''; consequently the accelerating force at M'' must act in the direction $M''C$.

23. Conceive a material point at M [Fig. 13], to be connected with a fixed point C by a thread MC

inextensible and without mass, and suppose it to receive an impulse in the direction MT at right angles with MC. In virtue of this impulse, it will describe the circumference of a circle of which the fixed point is the centre and MC the radius; and during the motion, the thread will suffer a certain tension in the direction of its length. But if we suppose applied to the point an accelerating force equal to this tension, and constantly directed towards the fixed centre C, we may consider the string withdrawn, and the point to be moving freely under the action of the primitive impulse and the accelerating force. Then as the areas described by the radius vector CM, in equal times, will be equal [Art. 21], the arcs described in equal times will also be equal, and the motion of the point will be uniform; and if we denote the velocity of the point by v, and by s the space described during the time t, we shall have

$$s = vt.$$

Let MN be the arc described by the material point during the infinitely small interval t', and denote the velocity of the point as before by v; then MN $= vt'$. The arc MN being infinitely small, the direction of the accelerating force may be supposed to remain parallel to MC while the point moves from M to N; and hence during the time t' this force may be regarded as constant in direction, as well as in intensity. If then the accelerating force were to act alone upon the point at M, it would cause it to describe the line MO during the time t'; and hence denoting the force by f, we shall have [Equa. 6]

$$MO = \tfrac{1}{2}ft'^2.$$

But considering the arc MN as coinciding with its chord, we have

$$MO \times MD = MN^2,$$

and hence $$MO = \frac{MN^2}{MD};$$

and denoting the radius MC by r, and substituting for MN its value vt', we have

$$MO = \frac{v^2t'^2}{2r}.$$

Hence we have $$\tfrac{1}{2}ft'^2 = \frac{v^2t'^2}{2r},$$

and $$f = \frac{v^2}{r}. \qquad [15]$$

The tension of the string to which the force f is equal and opposite, is called *the centrifugal force*, and f itself is called *the central* or *centripetal force;* each having for its measure the square of the velocity divided by the radius of the circle.

We have considered the radius CM constant; but we may suppose it to vary in length, so that the point shall describe any curve whatever. In that case the centrifugal force will vary from one point to another; but at any point of the curve, it will be equal to the square of the velocity divided by the radius of the osculating circle. For, the osculating circle at any point coinciding for an infinitely small space with the curve itself, the material point may be considered as moving, at each point of the curve, on the arc of the osculating circle at that point.

24. To find the relation between gravity and the centrifugal force, when the material point revolves on the circumference of a circle, let h be the height from which a body must fall in order to acquire the velocity v; then $v^2 = 2gh$, and substituting the value of v in equation [15],

$$f = \frac{v^2}{r},$$

we find
$$\frac{f}{g} = \frac{2h}{r},$$

that is, *the centrifugal force is to gravity, as twice the height due to the velocity of the material point, is to the radius of the circumference described by the point.*

25. If we denote by T the time in which a material point, moving uniformly with a velocity v, will describe the entire circumference of a circle of which the radius is r, we shall have

$$v = \frac{2\pi r}{T};$$

and substituting this value of v in the equation

$$f = \frac{v^2}{r},$$

we get
$$f = \frac{4\pi^2 r}{T^2}.$$

For a point which describes a circumference of which the radius is r', in the time T', we in like manner get

$$f' = \frac{4\pi^2 r'}{T'^2};$$

and hence we have

$$f : f' :: \frac{r}{T^2} : \frac{r'}{T'^2}, \quad \ldots\ldots\ldots\ldots [16]$$

that is, *the central forces in the two cases are directly as the radii, and inversely as the squares of the times.*

26. An illustration of the foregoing results is furnished by the revolution of the earth on its axis. Assuming the figure of the earth to be that of a sphere, let PP′ [Fig. 14] represent its axis, and the semi-circumference PEP′ the terrestrial meridian of any place M on its surface. From the centre C draw CE perpendicular to PP′, and draw MN parallel to it. Draw also CM. Then as PEP′ revolves, the point E will describe the equator, and M a parallel of latitude; and as each circle is described in the same time, denoting the centrifugal forces at E and M by f and f', and the latitude of the place by n, we shall have (proportion 16)

$$f : f' :: EC : MN,$$

$$:: EC : CM \,.\, \cos n,$$

or

$$f : f' :: 1 : \cos n,$$

and hence

$$f' = f \,.\, \cos n; \quad \ldots\ldots\ldots\ldots\ldots\ldots [17]$$

that is, *the centrifugal force at any place on the earth's surface, is equal to the centrifugal force at the equator, multiplied by the cosine of the latitude of the place.*

27. The effect of the centrifugal force due to the

rotation of the earth, is evidently to diminish the intensity of gravity at all points of the earth's surface except at the poles. At the equator, the centrifugal force and gravity are directly opposed to each other. Hence if we denote the intensity of gravity at the equator, as determined by observation, by g; the intensity which it would have, did the earth not revolve on its axis, by G, and the centrifugal force at the equator by f, we shall have

$$g = G - f, \quad \text{and } G = g + f.$$

The value of g has been found to be equal to $32,^{ft.}0861$. The general value of f [Art. 25], is given by the equation

$$f = \frac{4\pi^2 r}{T^2};$$

and for the case in question, we have r, or the equatorial radius of the earth = 20920300 feet; and T the sidereal day, or the time of the earth's revolution on its axis = 0,997269 of a mean solar day = 86164″ of mean solar time; and, hence, by substitution, we get

$$f = 0,^{ft.}1112. \quad \ldots\ldots\ldots\ldots\ldots\ldots \text{[a]}$$

We thus have

$$G = 32,^{ft.}0861 + 0,^{ft.}1112 = 32,^{ft.}1973, \quad \ldots\ldots\ldots \text{[b]}$$

28. Dividing equation [a] by [b], we get

$$\frac{f}{G} = \frac{0,^{ft.}1112}{32,^{ft.}1973} = \frac{1}{289}, \text{ and hence } f = \frac{1}{289} G;$$

that is, at the equator, the centrifugal force is the

$\frac{1}{289}$th of the intensity which gravity would have, had the earth no motion of rotation.

29. At any point of the earth's surface, not on the equator, the directions of gravity and the centrifugal force are oblique to each other. Thus at M [Fig. 14], gravity acts in the direction CR, and the centrifugal force in the direction NO. To determine the effect of the latter in the direction CR, let the centrifugal force be represented by the line MO, and be resolved into the components MR, MQ, the one in the line CR, the other at right angles to it; then denoting the latitude of M as before by n, we get

$$\text{MR} = \text{MO} \,.\, \cos n.$$

But [equa. 17] $\quad \text{MO} = f' = f \cos n,$

and hence $\quad \text{MR} = f \cos^2 n;$

that is, the diminution of gravity, due to the centrifugal force at any place on the earth's surface, is equal to the centrifugal force at the equator, multiplied by the square of the cosine of the latitude of the place.

Experiments with the pendulum show that the intensity of gravity at the poles exceeds the intensity at the equator by $\frac{1}{200}$th of G: of this increment, the $\frac{1}{289}$th is, as we have seen, due to the centrifugal force; the remainder is accounted for by the spheroidal figure of the earth.

30. As the centrifugal force depends upon the time of rotation, it may be proposed to determine in

what time the earth should revolve on its axis, in order that the centrifugal force may be equal to gravity. For the solution of this problem we have recourse to proportion [16,]

$$f : f' :: \frac{r}{T^2} : \frac{r'}{T'^2}.$$

In this proportion we make $r = r' =$ the equatorial radius of the earth, and we suppose T and T′ to represent respectively the present and required periods of rotation, and f and $f' =$ G the corresponding centrifugal forces. We thus get

$$f : G :: T'^2 : T^2,$$

and hence $$T' = \sqrt{\frac{f}{G}} . T;$$

or $$T' = \sqrt{\tfrac{1}{289}} . T = \tfrac{1}{17} . T.$$

Thus the required time is $\frac{1}{17}$th of the present period of rotation.

OF PROJECTILES.

31. A body moving near the surface of the earth, in virtue of a primitive impulse and the action of gravity, is called *a projectile.* In what follows, we shall consider the projectile as reduced to a material point, and the motion to take place in a vacuum.

Suppose then a material point, situated at A [Fig. 15], to receive an impulse in the direction AD, and then to be abandoned to the action of gravity. Let the space which it would describe in an instant in virtue of this impulse be represented by AD, and let the effect of gravity during the instant be represented by AE; then at the end of the first instant, the point will be found at B, having during the instant described the diagonal AB of the parallelogram constructed on AE and AD.

Again, on AB produced, take BG = AB; and on BG, and the vertical BF = AE, construct the parallelogram BFCG: at the end of the second instant, the point will be at C, having described the diagonal BC. In like manner, during the third instant, the point will describe the side CH; during the fourth, the side HI, and so on. But each diagonal being infinitely small, the series of diagonals forms a curve; and since each of the parallelograms has its contiguous sides in the vertical plane which contains the preceding parallelogram, all the points of this curve are in the same vertical plane. This curve is called *the trajectory* of the material point.

32. To find the equation of the trajectory, through the point A [Fig. 16] from which the material point is projected, draw the axes AX, AY, horizontal and vertical respectively. Let AK be the direction of the primitive impulse, and denote the velocity due to the impulse by v. Let the curve described be represented by AMC, and let M be the position of the point at the end of the time t. Draw MP perpendicular to AX, and produce it to M′. Put $AP = x$, $PM = y$, and the angle $M'AP = i$. Then let the

initial velocity v, represented by AM″, be resolved into the components

$$AP' = v \cos i, \text{ and } AQ = v \sin i.$$

The material point may evidently be regarded as having two motions, the one parallel to AX, the other to AY. The motion parallel to AY is the same as that of a body projected vertically upwards with a velocity $v \sin i$; and hence we have [Art. 9],

$$y = v \sin i \, t - \tfrac{1}{2}gt^2. \quad\ldots\ldots\ldots\ldots [18]$$

The other is due to the horizontal component $v \cos i$, and gives

$$x = v \cos i \, t,$$

or

$$t = \frac{x}{v \cos i}.$$

Substituting this value of t in equation [18], and putting $2gh$ in place of v^2 [Art. 8, equa. 9], we get

$$4hy \cos^2 i = 4hx \sin i \cos i - x^2; \quad\ldots\ldots\ldots [19]$$

and hence,

$$x = 2h \sin i \cos i \pm \sqrt{4h \cos^2 i \, (h \sin^2 i - y)}. \quad\ldots [20]$$

33. The distance from the origin A to the point C, where the curve intersects the horizontal line AX, is technically called *the range*. To determine its value, in equation [20], we make $y = 0$: we thus get

$$\begin{aligned} AC &= 4h \sin i \cos i \\ &= 2h \, 2\sin i \cos i \\ &= 2h \sin 2i. \quad\ldots\ldots\ldots\ldots [21] \end{aligned}$$

This is the general expression for the range.

When $i = 45°$, or $2i = 90°$, we have

$$AC = 2h.$$

This is evidently the maximum value of AC. Hence, for a given initial velocity, the range is greatest when the angle of projection is equal to 45°. Denoting this value of the range by R', we have

$$R' = 2h,$$

and hence $$h = \frac{R'}{2};$$

from which it appears that the height due to the initial velocity is equal to half the maximum range. Hence, to determine h, we have only to measure the range when the angle of projection is 45°.

34. Resuming equation [21], and denoting AC by R, we have

$$R = 2h \sin 2i;$$

and substituting for $2h$ its value R', we have

$$R = R' \sin 2i,$$

an equation which gives the range corresponding to any angle of projection, when the maximum range for the same initial velocity is known.

35. Let us now suppose two material points to be projected with equal initial velocities, and denote the angles of projection by i' and i'', and the corresponding ranges by R''' and R^{IV}. We have, equa. [21],

$$R''' = 2h \sin 2i',$$

$$R^{IV} = 2h \sin 2i'';$$

and if $i'' = (90° - i')$, we get

$$R^{\text{IV}} = 2h \sin(180° - 2i')$$
$$= 2h \sin 2i',$$

and $$R''' = R^{\text{IV}};$$

that is, when two material points are projected with equal initial velocities, at angles of projection which are complementary to each other, the range is the same for each.

36. From equation [20], we learn that the greatest elevation of the point, or the maximum value of y, is $h \sin^2 i$; for if y be greater than $h \sin^2 i$, the radical becomes imaginary. The value of x corresponding to the maximum value of y, is $2h \sin i \cos i$. Supposing AE and ED to be these values, we have

$$\text{AE} = 2h \sin i \cos i,$$
$$\text{ED} = h \sin^2 i.$$

37. If, when the initial velocity is given, it be required to determine what must be the value of the angle of projection, in order that the projectile may reach a given point N, for which we have

$$x = \text{AQ}' = x', \text{ and } y = \text{Q'N} = y',$$

we have recourse to equation [19]. Substituting in this equation the given values of x and y, and dividing each member by $\cos^2 i$, we get

$$4hy' = 4hx' \frac{\sin i}{\cos i} - \frac{x'^2}{\cos^2 i};$$

and since $$\frac{1}{\cos^2 i} = \sec^2 i = 1 + \text{tang}^2 i,$$

we have $$4hy' = 4hx' \text{ tang } i - x'^2 - x'^2 \text{ tang}^2 i,$$

or $$\text{tang}^2 i - \frac{4h}{x'} \text{tang}\, i = \frac{-4hy' - x'^2}{x'^2};$$

and hence $$\text{tang}\, i = \frac{2h \pm \sqrt{4h^2 - 4hy' - x'^2}}{x'}.$$

We learn from this equation, that in order that the problem may be possible, we must have

$$4hy' + x'^2 < 4h^2;$$

and that when this condition is satisfied, there are two directions in which the projectile may be thrown, so as to reach the given point.

38. The time employed by the projectile in describing any portion of the trajectory, may be found from the equation

$$x = v \cos i\, t.$$

39. In equation [19], the points of the curve are referred to the axes AX, AY. Let us now refer them to the axes DE and DY′ [Fig. 17], drawn through D, the highest point of the trajectory, parallel to AY and AX respectively. Denote DR, the new abscissa of the point M, by x'; and MR, the new ordinate, by y': we have [Art. 36]

$$x = 2h \sin i \cos i - y',$$

and $$y = h \sin^2 i - x'.$$

Substituting these values of x and y in equation [19]

$$4hy \cos^2 i = 4hx \sin i \cos i - x^2,$$

we have

$$4h\,(h \sin^2 i - x') \cos^2 i = 4h\,(2h \sin i \cos i - y') \sin i \cos i - (2h \sin i \cos i - y')^2;$$

or, reducing,

$$4h^2 \sin^2 i \cos^2 i - 4h \cos^2 i\, x' = 8h^2 \sin^2 i \cos^2 i - 4h \sin i \cos i\, y' \\ - 4h^2 \sin^2 i \cos^2 i + 4h \sin i \cos i\, y' - y'^2,$$

and, by a farther reduction,

$$y'^2 = 4h \cos^2 i\, x'.$$

From this equation, it appears that the trajectory is a parabola, having its vertex at D, and of which the parameter to the axis is $4h \cos^2 i$.*

MEASURE OF FORCES.

40. In article 8 of Part First, we have shown how the intensities of forces may be represented by algebraic symbols; and assuming the forces to act upon single material particles, we have also shown that the spaces described by different particles in the same time, or their velocities, are directly proportional to the intensities of the forces; and, conversely, that the forces are directly as the velocities. Thus denoting the forces which act separately upon two material particles by f and f', and the velocities which they communicate to the particles by v and v', we have shown that

$$f : f' :: v : v'. \quad \text{[a]}$$

1° Let us now substitute for the particles, two

* That the trajectory is a parabola, may also be shown by referring the points of the curve to the oblique co-ordinates AX, AK. The method in the text is employed, because it illustrates the simplification which frequently results from a change of co-ordinates.

bodies of equal masses, each body consisting of M particles; and let us suppose each particle of the first to be acted upon by a force equal to f, and each particle of the second by a force equal to f'; the impulses being supposed to be given in the same sense, and in parallel directions. The bodies will evidently move with the velocities v and v' (all their particles describing parallel straight lines); and their motions may be considered as due directly to the resultants, equal respectively to Mf and Mf', of the M equal and parallel components which act upon the particles of each body. Denoting these resultants by Q and Q', we have

$$Q = Mf, \text{ and } Q' = Mf';$$

and hence

$$Q : Q' :: Mf : Mf'$$
$$:: f : f',$$

or, equa. [a], $Q : Q' :: v : v'$. .... [b]

Thus the intensities of any two forces are to each other as the velocities which they would respectively communicate to two bodies of the same mass; or, more briefly, when the masses are equal, the forces are as the velocities.

2° Referring again to the two bodies, let us suppose them to have unequal masses, the one to have a mass m, the other a mass M; and let us conceive each of their particles to be acted upon by a force equal to f. The bodies will evidently move with the common velocity v; and their motions may be considered as due to the resultants, equal to mf and

Mf respectively, of the parallel components which act upon their particles. Denoting these components by F and Q respectively, we shall have

$$F : Q :: mf : Mf$$
$$:: m : M. \ldots\ldots\ldots\ldots [c]$$

Thus any two forces are to each other as the masses to which, if respectively applied, they would communicate equal velocities; or when the velocities are equal, the forces are as the masses.

3° Having ascertained the relation between the intensities of two forces, 1st, When the forces communicate unequal velocities to equal masses, and, 2d, When they communicate equal velocities to unequal masses, we will now consider the general case, that in which the forces communicate unequal velocities to unequal masses.

Let F and F' denote the forces, m and m' the masses, and v and v' the velocities respectively. Also let Q and Q' denote two auxiliary forces, whose intensities are such that they would communicate to two bodies of the same mass M the velocities v and v' respectively.

We have [1° of this Art.],

$$Q : Q' :: v : v'.$$

We also have [2° of this Art.]

$$F : Q :: m : M,$$
$$F' : Q' :: m' : M;$$

and eliminating the quantities Q, Q' and M, we get

$$F : F' :: mv : m'v'. \ldots\ldots\ldots\ldots [d]$$

The product of the mass m of a body by its velocity v, is called *the quantity of motion* of the body. Employing this term, the proportion just found may be thus enunciated:

Two forces are in general to each other as the quantities of motion which they would respectively generate in any two bodies during the same time.

4° If in proportion [d] we suppose m' to become the unit of mass, and v' the unit of velocity, F' will become the force which will communicate to the unit of mass a velocity equal to the unit of velocity; and if we take it for the unit of force, we shall have

$$F = mv, \qquad \text{[e]}$$

mv being the ratio of the force F to the unit of force.

5° If in proportion [d] we suppose $F = F'$, we get $mv = m'v'$, and hence

$$v = \frac{m'v'}{m}. \qquad \text{[h]}$$

Thus the quantity of motion $m'v'$ due to a force F being given, to find the velocity which the same force would communicate to a body whose mass is m, we have only to divide the given quantity of motion by this mass.

6° The preceding relations are evidently true, whatever the value of v: whether it be a finite velocity, due to a force of the kind called impulsive; or an infinitely small velocity, such as we conceive a force acting at infinitely small intervals, like gravity, to communicate at the commencement of each interval; or, lastly, whether it be the finite velocity produced by the latter kind of force, that is, an accelerating force acting during a given time.

Reserving v to denote the velocity due to an impulsive force, and employing φ to denote the velocity due to an accelerating force acting uniformly during the unit of time, we shall have, for the two cases,

$$F = mv, \qquad [k]$$

$$F = m\varphi. \qquad [k']$$

If in these equations we make $m = 1$, we get

$$F = v, \quad F = \varphi;$$

and F becomes in each case the force which acts upon a material particle, or the unit of mass. For the sake of brevity, φ is commonly called *the accelerating force;* and $m\varphi$ the general expression of F in equation [k'], is called *the moving force.*

41. *Nature of an impulsive force.*

We learn from experiment, that in all cases of collision, the bodies concerned suffer a sensible compression, of greater or less extent, according to their degree of hardness. This compression is evidently effected in a finite, though very short time, and by infinitely small degrees. Hence in the production of motion by an impulsive force, we may conceive the transmission of the motion from the one body to the other also to take place by infinitely small degrees. Thus in this case, as in that of an accelerating or moving force, we may conceive the time during which the force acts, to be divided into an infinite number of instants, and suppose an infinitely small velocity to be communicated at the commencement of each instant; the essential difference in the two cases being that the infinitesimal velocities communicated by the impulsive force must be supposed to be vastly greater than those communicated by the moving force. *An impulsive force may therefore be regarded as a moving force, acting for a very short time, with a very great intensity.* Since then the finite impulse given by an impulsive force may be supposed to be made up of an infinite number of infinitely small impulses, we may simplify our first notion of the mode of action of a force (Art. 2 of Statics), and say that the action of a force may always be conceived to consist in communicating to the particles of the body on which it acts, infinitely small impulses of greater or less intensity.

42. To give a simple example of the application of some of the preceding results (Art. 40), let m and m' denote the masses of two bodies, suspended at the extremities of a cord which passes over a fixed pulley, and let the velocity which gravity will communicate to the bodies during a unit of time be denoted by g. The moving forces put in operation by this disposition of the bodies will be mg and $m'g$; and supposing $m > m'$, their resultant will be $mg - m'g$. This resultant, acting upon the sum $(m + m')$ of the two masses, will cause the one body to descend, the other to ascend; and the velocity g' which it will communicate to the system in the unit of time, will be given (5° of this Art.) by the equation

$$g' = \frac{m - m'}{m + m'} g.$$

The simple arrangement just considered, is the skeleton of a machine called, from the name of its inventor, *Atwood's machine;* in which, by rendering the difference between the masses sufficiently small, the motion of the bodies is rendered so slow that the velocity acquired, and the space described, in any given time, can be determined by actual observation. It has thus been found that bodies near the surface of the earth fall with a uniformly accelerated motion, and hence that terrestrial gravity is *a constant accelerating force.*

PRINCIPLE OF D'ALEMBERT.

43. In the preceding sections, we have constantly supposed the body whose motion was the subject of investigation, to be reduced to a single material point. We purpose now to consider some of the more elementary cases of the motion of systems of points, or bodies of sensible magnitude. But the student must first be made acquainted with a general principle of great utility in the solution of problems of dynamics, called, from the name of its discoverer, *the principle of D'Alembert.*

Let A, B, C, D, etc. [Fig. 18], be a system of material points, connected with each other in any manner whatever, and acted upon by the accelerating forces f, f', f'', f''', etc. respectively. The velocities which the points will actually acquire in an infinitely small time or *instant,* under the action of these forces, will, in consequence of their mutual connexion, be different in both intensity and direction from those which they would acquire were they free. Thus if the velocity which f would communicate to A in an instant if that point were free, be represented by AC, the velocity actually acquired by A will, in consequence of the connexion of the points of the system, be represented by some other line AD. Let the velocity AD be considered a component of AC, and let the parallelogram ABCD be completed: we shall then have the velocity AC resolved into the two velocities AD and AB. To distinguish these velocities from each other, we call AC the *impressed velocity*, AD the *effective velocity*, and AB the *velocity lost*. Let the velocity which f would communicate to A in the unit of time if it were free, be denoted by u; then the velocity which it would communicate in the instant t', or the impressed velocity, will be expressed by ut'; and if we denote the components of u by q and p, the effective velocity and the velocity lost will be expressed by qt and pt respectively. If moreover we denote the mass of the point A by m, then for this point

the impressed quantity of motion will be expressed by mut';

the effective quantity of motion by .... mqt',

and the quantity of motion lost by .... mpt'.

If for the points B, C, D, etc., we denote the quantities corresponding to u, q, p and m, by these letters accented, that is, by u', q', p', m'; u'', q'', p'', m'', etc., the several quantities of motion for the entire system will be thus expressed:

The impressed quantities of motion by

mut', $m'u't'$, $m''u''t'$, etc.; .... [a]

the effective quantities of motion by

$$mqt', \quad m'q't', \quad m''q''t', \text{ etc.}; \quad \ldots\ldots\ldots\ldots [b]$$

the quantities of motion lost by

$$mpt', \quad m'p't', \quad m''p''t', \text{ etc.} \quad \ldots\ldots\ldots\ldots [c]$$

Now since the impressed quantities of motion are reduced, in consequence of the mutual connexion of the points, to the effective quantities of motion, it is obvious that *the quantities of motion lost must be in equilibrium among themselves.* In this consists the principle of D'Alembert. The manner in which the equilibrium will take place, will of course depend upon the nature of the system.

44. This principle may also be enunciated in terms of the impressed and effective quantities of motion. To get this latter enunciation, produce DA: and taking AD′ equal to AD, complete the parallelogram ACBD′. We perceive that AB the velocity lost is the resultant of AC the impressed velocity, and AD′ the effective velocity taken contrary to the actual direction of the motion. Thus for the point A, the quantity of motion lost may be resolved into the impressed quantity of motion, and the effective quantity of motion, the latter being taken contrary to its actual direction. The same being true for all the points of the system, we may substitute for the quantities of motion [c], the quantities of motion [a] and [b], the latter [b] being taken with the above modification. But the quantities of motion [c] are in equilibrium among themselves: consequently an equilibrium must also exist between the quantities of motion [a] and [b], the latter being

taken contrary to the actual motions. *Thus, in any system whatever, there will be an equilibrium between the impressed and effective quantities of motion, the latter being taken contrary to the actual motions;* regard being had, in forming the equations of equilibrium, to the nature of the system.

This enunciation might have been obtained independently of the former; for the truth of it is obvious, the moment the terms *impressed and effective quantities of motion* are understood in the sense in which they are here used. The preceding method has been employed to ensure a greater familiarity with the principle, than could be acquired by regarding it from a single point of view.

We have supposed the particles of the system to be acted upon by accelerating forces only, but the principle is equally true when the forces are impulsive.

MOMENT OF INERTIA.

45. The sum of the products obtained by multiplying the masses of the particles of a body by the squares of their respective distances from any line whatever, is called *the moment of inertia* of the body with respect to the line.

The moment of inertia of a body is represented by the expression $\Sigma(r^2m)$; in which m denotes the mass of a particle of the body, and r the distance of the particle from the axis with respect to which the moment is taken. When the moment of inertia of a body with respect to an axis which passes through its centre of gravity is known, its moment of inertia with respect to any other axis can be readily determined.

Let C [Fig. 19] be the centre of gravity of the body, and FF′ an axis passing through it, with respect to which the moment of inertia of the body is known: and let its moment of inertia with respect to any other axis KK′, parallel to FF′, be required. Let the point C be taken for the origin of co-ordinates, and the axis FF′ for the axis of z; and let CX and CY, the axes of x and y, be drawn. Let N be the place of any particle of the body, and draw through it the plane NKF parallel to the plane of xy, and meeting the axes of moments in the points F and K. Draw NE perpendicular to the plane of xy, EP and GD perpendicular to the axis of x, and ED′ parallel to that axis; and join the points C and E, C and G, E and G. Let CD and DG, the co-ordinates of G, be denoted by α and β; CP and PE, the co-ordinates of E, by x and y; and CG, the distance between the two axes, by a. Also let NK = EG be denoted by r, and NF = EC by $r_{,}$. We have

$$CG^2 = CD^2 + DG^2, \text{ and } CE^2 = CP^2 + PE^2;$$

or $$a^2 = \alpha^2 + \beta^2, \text{ and } r_{,}^2 = x^2 + y^2 \ldots\ldots\ldots \text{[a]}$$

We also have

$$EG^2 = ED'^2 + D'G^2,$$

or $$r^2 = (x - \alpha)^2 + (\beta - y)^2$$

$$= x^2 - 2\alpha x + \alpha^2 + \beta^2 - 2\beta y + y^2;$$

or, reducing by equations [a],

$$r^2 = r'^2 - 2\alpha x - 2\beta y + a^2;$$

and multiplying each member of this equation by the mass m of the particle, we get

$$r^2m = r_,^2m - 2\alpha xm - 2\beta ym + a^2m.$$

If, for other particles of the system, we denote the quantities corresponding to r, $r_,$, x and y, by these letters accented, we shall have

$$r'^2m = r_{,,}^2m - 2\alpha x'm - 2\beta y'm + a^2m,$$

$$r''^2m = r_{,,,}^2m - 2\alpha x''m - 2\beta y''m + a^2m,$$

etc.;

and adding these equations, supposed to extend to all the particles of the body, we shall get

$$\Sigma(r^2m) = \Sigma(r_,^2m) - 2\alpha\Sigma(xm) - 2\beta\Sigma(ym) + a^2\Sigma m.$$

Now $\Sigma(xm)$ is the sum of the moments of the masses of the particles with respect to the plane of yz, which passes through the centre of gravity of the body; and hence we have $\Sigma(xm) = 0$. For a similar reason, we have $\Sigma(ym) = 0$. Also Σm expresses the sum of the masses of all the particles of the body, or its entire mass M. Consequently we have

$$\Sigma(r^2m) = \Sigma(r_,^2m) + a^2M. \qquad \text{[b]}$$

In this equation, the term $\Sigma(r_,^2m)$ expresses the moment of inertia of the body with respect to the axis FF′ which passes through its centre of gravity; and $\Sigma(r^2m)$ expresses its moment of inertia with respect to the axis KK′ parallel to the first axis, and at a distance from it equal to a. Hence *the moment of inertia of a body with respect to any axis, is equal to its moment of inertia with respect to an axis passing through its centre of gravity, parallel to the first, plus the product of the mass of the body by the square of the distance between the two axes.*

The second member of equation [b] may be put under the form

$$M\left(\frac{\Sigma(r_{\prime}^{2}m)}{M}+a^2\right).$$

Hence we have

$$\Sigma(r^2m)=M\left(\frac{\Sigma(r_{\prime}^{2}m)}{M}+a^2\right);$$

or, denoting

$$\frac{\Sigma(r_{\prime}^{2}m)}{M} \text{ by } k^2,$$

$$\Sigma(r^2m)=M(k^2+a^2.) \quad\ldots\ldots\ldots\ldots\ldots\ldots [c]$$

46. The determination of the moments of inertia of particular bodies requires in general the use of the integral calculus, but in many cases they can be found by more elementary processes. We will give a few examples.

1° *The straight line.*

Let it be required to find the moment of inertia of a material straight line, with respect to an axis which passes through the centre of gravity of the line, at right angles to it.

Let AB [Fig. 20] be the line, and C its centre of gravity; and let it be supposed to be divided into $2n$ indefinitely small equal parts or elements, by sections perpendicular to its length. Let its length be denoted by l, and the area of a section by s. The volume of an element will be expressed by $\frac{sl}{2n}$; and as the mass is here supposed to be proportional to the volume, we may also take this expression as the measure of the mass of the element. Moreover the respective distances of the elements of BC (half of the line) from C, that is, from the axis of moments, will be expressed by

$$\frac{l}{2n},\ 2.\frac{l}{2n},\ 3.\frac{l}{2n},\ \ldots\ldots\ldots\ldots\ n.\frac{l}{2n}.$$

Consequently the moment of inertia of BC will be

$$\frac{sl}{2n}\cdot\left(\frac{l}{2n}\right)^2 + \frac{sl}{2n}\cdot\left(\frac{2l}{2n}\right)^2 + \ldots\ldots\ldots + \frac{sl}{2n}\cdot\left(\frac{nl}{2n}\right)^2,$$

or $$\frac{sl}{2n}\cdot\left(\frac{l}{2n}\right)^2 (1^2 + 2^2 + 3^2 + \ldots\ldots n^2),$$

or $$\frac{sl^3}{8}\cdot\frac{1}{n^3}\left(\frac{n^3}{3} + \frac{n^2}{2} + \frac{n}{6}\right),*$$

*To find the sum of the series

$$1^2 + 2^2 + 3^2 \ldots\ldots\ldots\ldots\ldots\ldots + n^2:$$

in the identical equation

$$(x-1)^3 = (x-1)^3,$$

or $$(x-1)^3 = x^3 - 3x^2 + 3x - 1:$$

substitute successively for x each term of the series

$$1,\ 2,\ 3,\ 4, \ldots\ldots\ldots\ldots n.$$

We shall thus get the following equations:

$$0 = 1^3 - 3.1^2 + 3.1 - 1,$$
$$1^3 = 2^3 - 3.2^2 + 3.2 - 1,$$
$$2^3 = 3^3 - 3.3^2 + 3.3 - 1,$$
$$\ldots\ldots\ldots\ldots\ldots\ldots\ldots\ldots,$$
$$(n-2)^3 = (n-1)^3 - 3(n-1)^2 + 3(n-1) - 1,$$
$$(n-1)^3 = n^3 - 3n^2 + 3n - 1;$$

and if we add the corresponding terms, cancelling those which are common, and denoting the sum of the series $1 + 2 + 3 + 4 \ldots\ldots + n$

or (since we must suppose $n = \infty$)

$$\frac{sl^3}{24}.$$

Hence the moment of inertia of the entire line will be expressed by $\frac{sl^3}{12}$; or, denoting the mass of the line by M, by $M\frac{l^2}{12}$.

The moment of inertia of AB with respect to any other axis parallel to the first, and at a distance from it denoted by a, will be expressed [Art. 45] by

$$M\left(\frac{M\frac{l^2}{12}}{M} + a^2\right).$$

2° *The rectangle.*

Let it be required to determine the moment of inertia of an infinitely thin rectangular plate.

1st. Let ABDE [Fig. 21] be the plate, and let the axis HI with respect to which the moment is to be taken be supposed to pass through C the centre of gravity of the plate, and to be *parallel to one of its sides,* as AB. Conceive the plate to be made up of

by s', and that of the series $1^2 + 2^2 + 3^2 + 4^2 \ldots\ldots + n^2$ by s'', we shall have

$$0 = n^3 - 3\,s'' + 3\,s' - n;$$

and hence

$$s'' = \frac{n^3}{3} + s' - \frac{n}{3}$$

$$= \frac{n^3}{3} + (n+1)\frac{n}{2} - \frac{n}{3}$$

$$= \frac{n^3}{3} + \frac{n^2}{2} + \frac{n}{6}.$$

material lines perpendicular to HI. The moment of inertia of each line with respect to this axis will be expressed by $M\frac{l^2}{12}$, M denoting the mass of the line and l its length. Hence if we suppose M to denote the sum of the masses of the lines, or the mass of the entire plate, the moment of inertia required will be expressed by $M\frac{l^2}{12}$.

2d. Let the axis be supposed to pass through C, *at right angles to the surface of the plate.* As in the preceding case, conceive the plane to be made up of material lines or elements parallel to the side AE: and let the number of these elements, or the indefinitely small equal parts into which we suppose the line AB to be divided, be denoted by $2n$. Let AB and AE be denoted by b and l respectively, and the thickness of the plate by i. The volume, and hence the mass of each element, will be measured by $\frac{bli}{2n}$; and the moment of inertia of an element will be expressed by

$$\frac{bli}{2n}\left\{\frac{\frac{bli}{2n}\cdot\frac{l^2}{12}}{\frac{bli}{2n}}+\left(p\cdot\frac{b}{2n}\right)^2\right\},$$

p being any number of the natural series. Hence the sum of the moments of inertia of all the lines composing the semi-rectangle ALKE will be

$$\frac{bli}{2n}\left(\frac{l^2}{12}+\left(\frac{b}{2n}\right)^2\right)+\frac{bli}{2n}\left(\frac{l^2}{12}+\left(\frac{2b}{2n}\right)^2\right)+\ldots+\frac{bli}{2n}\left(\frac{l^2}{12}+\left(\frac{nb}{2n}\right)^2\right).$$

or $$\frac{bli}{2n}\left(\frac{nl^2}{12}+\left(\frac{b}{2n}\right)^2(1^2+2^2+3^2+\ldots\ldots+n^2)\right),$$

or $$\frac{bli}{2n}\left(\frac{nl^2}{12}+\left(\frac{b}{2n}\right)^2\cdot\left(\frac{n^3}{3}+\frac{n^2}{2}+\frac{n}{6}\right)\right),$$

or $$\frac{bli}{2}\left(\frac{l^2}{12}+\frac{b^2}{4}\cdot\frac{1}{n^3}\cdot\left(\frac{n^3}{3}+\frac{n^2}{2}+\frac{n}{6}\right)\right),$$

or $$\frac{bli}{2}\left(\frac{l^2+b^2}{12}\right).$$

Consequently the moment of inertia of the entire rectangle, its mass being denoted by M and its diagonal by d, will be expressed by $M\frac{d^2}{12}$.

3° *The rectangular parallelopipedon and triangular prism.*

Since a rectangular parallelopipedon [Fig. 22] may be supposed to be made up of a series of equal rectangular plates, its moment of inertia with respect to an axis CC′ passing through the centres of gravity of any two of its opposite faces will be expressed by the formula $M\frac{d^2}{12}$; M being supposed to denote the mass of the solid, and d the diagonal of either of the faces to which the axis is perpendicular.

The same formula also expresses the moment of inertia of either of the equal triangular prisms into which the parallelopipedon is divided by the diagonal plane ADD′A′, with respect to the axis CC′ which joins the middle points of the hypothenuses AD and A′D′ of their triangular bases; M being supposed to denote the mass of either of the two prisms, and d the hypothenuse AD or A′D′.

THE COMPOUND PENDULUM.

47. The simple pendulum has only an ideal existence. It is essential, therefore, to the practical application of the results obtained in articles 19 and 20, relative to this pendulum, that the relations between it and the compound pendulum should be known. These relations we are now to investigate.

Let a compound pendulum be conceived to oscillate about a horizontal axis. During its motion, the material points, or particles of which it is composed, will describe arcs of circles, the planes of which will be perpendicular to the axis. Let OGFH [Fig. 23] be one of these planes, and O the point in which it is intersected by the axis; the axis being supposed to be perpendicular to the plane of the paper.

The pendulum being in motion, suppose that at the expiration of the time t, the particle which describes the arc HFG has arrived at the point A, having during that time described the arc HA. Denote by ω the *angular velocity* of the whole system at this instant; that is, the velocity of any point, as I, at the distance from the axis which we assume as the linear unit; and denote the distance OA by r: then the absolute velocity of the element at A will be expressed by $r\omega$. In the following instant, this velocity will be increased by the action of gravity. Let g the intensity of gravity be represented by the vertical line AD, and be resolved into the two components AE and AB, the one in the direction of OA, and the other perpendicular to it. The first being destroyed by the re-action of the fixed point C, we have to consider only the latter. This component causes the angular velocity to vary, and, if we represent the angle BAD by δ, will be expressed by $g \cos\delta$. If we denote the increment which the angular velocity receives during the instant t', by ω', the corresponding increment of the velocity of the particle at A will be expressed by $r\omega'$; and at the end of the time $t+t'$, the velocity of the particle will be expressed by $r\omega + r\omega'$.

If the element at A were unconnected with the other particles of the system, the accelerating force $g \cos\delta$ would communicate to it, during the instant t', the velocity $g \cos\delta\, t'$; and at the end of the time $t+t'$, its velocity would be $r\omega + g \cos\delta\, t'$; the direction of the velocity being AB, the same as at the end of the time t.

Now these increments of velocity $g \cos\delta\, t'$ and $r\omega'$ are what we have called, in Art. 43, *impressed* and *effective velocities* respectively. Hence denoting the mass of the particle at A by m, the impressed quantity of motion of this particle will be $g \cos\delta\, t'm$, and its effective quantity of motion $r\omega'm$. All that we have shown to be true of the particle at A, being equally true of all the other particles of the system, we shall have for the impressed quantities of motion of the whole system a series of terms each of the form $g \cos\delta\, t'm$, the sum of which, employing the usual symbol, may be expressed by

$$\Sigma(g \cos\delta\, t'm).$$

We shall also have for the effective quantity of motion of the system a series of terms of the form $r\omega' m$, the sum of which may be expressed by

$$\Sigma(r\omega' m).$$

Now according to the principle of D'Alembert [Art. 44], these two quantities of motion will be in equilibrium with each other, if the latter be taken in directions contrary to the actual directions of the motions. The case then is exactly similar to that of Art. 40 of Statics; and the condition of equilibrium is, that the sum of the moments of the forces which tend to turn the system in one sense about the fixed axis, must be equal to the sum of the moments of the forces which tend to turn the system in the opposite sense, the moments being taken with respect to the axis itself.

To obtain the moments of the forces or quantities of motion, we have only to multiply the quantities of motion (impressed and effective) of each element, by the distance of the element from the axis. We shall thus get for the equation of equilibrium,

$$\Sigma(r^2\omega' m) = \Sigma(rg \cos\delta \; t' m) ;$$

or since ω' is common to all the terms of the first member, and t' and g to those of the second,

$$\omega'\Sigma(r^2 m) = gt'\Sigma(r \cos\delta \; m) ;$$

and hence we shall have

$$\frac{\omega'}{t'} = g\,\frac{\Sigma(r \cos\delta \; m)}{\Sigma(r^2 m)}.$$

Conceive now a vertical plane to be drawn through the fixed axis, and perpendiculars to be drawn to it from all the particles of the pendulum. Let AN $= y$ be the perpendicular drawn from the particle at A; then we shall have

$$y = r \cos \delta;$$

and hence, substituting y in place of $r \cos\delta$ in the preceding equation, we shall get

$$\frac{\omega'}{t'} = g \frac{\Sigma(ym)}{\Sigma(r^2m)}. \quad \ldots\ldots\ldots\ldots\ldots\ldots \quad [a]$$

The expression $\Sigma(ym)$ represents the sum of the moments of all the particles of the pendulum with respect to the vertical plane drawn through the axis; and if we denote by y' the perpendicular drawn from the centre of gravity of the pendulum to this plane, and by M the entire mass of the pendulum, we shall have [Statics, Art. 45],

$$\Sigma(ym) = y'M;$$

and hence

$$\frac{\omega'}{t'} = g \frac{y'M}{\Sigma(r^2m)}. \quad \ldots\ldots\ldots\ldots\ldots\ldots \quad [b]$$

Let C [Fig. 24] be the centre of gravity of the pendulum, and O′G′F′H′ the plane drawn through it perpendicular to the axis, and let O′ be the point of intersection of the plane and axis; then the line CN′, drawn perpendicular to the vertical O′F′, will be the line which we have denoted by y'; and denoting O′C by a, and the angle O′CN′ by δ', we shall have

$$y' = a \cos \delta'.$$

We also have [Art. 45],

$$\Sigma(r^2m) = M(a^2 + k^2).$$

Hence, by substitution, equation [b] will become

$$\frac{\omega'}{t'} = \frac{ga \cos \delta' M}{M(a^2 + k^2)} = \frac{ga \cos \delta'}{a^2 + k^2}.$$

The second member of this equation is obviously [Art. 10] the expression of the angular accelerating force for the whole pendulum.

Let us now seek the expression of the angular accelerating force for a single particle, situated at R on O′C produced; O′R being supposed to be without mass, and inextensible and inflexible, so that the line and particle together constitute a simple pendulum.

On the supposition that the compound pendulum is reduced to a single particle, equation [a] becomes

$$\frac{\omega'}{t'} = \frac{gym}{r^2m};$$

and applying this result to the particle at R, and denoting the line O′R by l, we get

$$\frac{\omega'}{t'} = \frac{gl \cos \delta'}{l^2}$$

$$= \frac{g \cos \delta'}{l}.$$

The second member of this equation is the expression required.

48. If now it be proposed to determine the value that must be given to l, in order that the simple pendulum (or the point at R) may oscillate in the

same time as the compound pendulum, we have only to put the expressions of the accelerating forces in the two cases equal to each other. We thus get

$$\frac{ga \cos \delta'}{a^2 + k^2} = \frac{g \cos \delta'}{l};$$

and hence $$\frac{a}{a^2 + k^2} = \frac{1}{l},$$

and $$l = \frac{a^2 + k^2}{a}$$

$$= a + \frac{k^2}{a}.$$

49. To apply this formula to a particular case, we must determine the mass M of the given pendulum, and the distance a of its centre of gravity from the axis of suspension. We must also calculate the moment of inertia of this mass, with respect to the axis passing through the centre of gravity parallel to the axis of suspension. Then dividing this moment by the mass, we shall have the value of k^2; and substituting the values of a and k^2 in the second member of the equation, we shall have the length l of the simple pendulum which will oscillate in the same time with the compound pendulum.

If through R, considered as a point of the compound pendulum, a line be drawn parallel to the axis of suspension, all the points of the line will obviously oscillate in the same manner as the point R. This line is called *the axis of oscillation* of the pendulum, and the points O′ and R are called *the centres of suspension and oscillation* respectively.

50. *The axes of oscillation and suspension are reciprocal; that is, when the axis of oscillation is made the axis of suspension, the latter becomes the axis of oscillation.*

For let AB [Fig. 25] be the section of a compound pendulum by a plane passing through its centre of gravity, perpendicular to the axis of suspension; and suppose C to be the centre of gravity, and O′ the centre of suspension. To determine the length of the corresponding simple pendulum, we have the equation

$$l = a + \frac{k^2}{a};$$

or, since $a = \text{O}'\text{C}$,

$$l = \text{O}'\text{C} + \frac{k^2}{\text{O}'\text{C}}.$$

If then on O′C produced we lay off CR equal to $\frac{k^2}{\text{O}'\text{C}}$, the point R will be the centre of oscillation.

Now let the pendulum be inverted, and the point R [Fig. 26] be taken for the centre of suspension: then denoting the length of the corresponding simple pendulum by l', and the distance between the centres of gravity and suspension by a', we have

$$l' = a' + \frac{k^2}{a'}$$

$$= \text{CR} + \frac{k^2}{\text{CR}};$$

or, since $\text{CR} = \frac{k^2}{\text{O}'\text{C}}$,

$$l' = \frac{k^2}{O'C} + \frac{k^2}{\frac{k^2}{O'C}}$$

$$= O'C + \frac{k^2}{O'C}.$$

Hence $$l = l'.$$

Thus the lengths of the corresponding simple pendulums are the same, and the oscillations about the axes of suspension and oscillation are made in equal times.

51. Conversely, *if the duration of the oscillations of a compound pendulum is the same about two parallel axes which lie in the same plane with the centre of gravity of the pendulum, and at unequal distances from that point, the distance between the axes will be equal to the length of the simple pendulum which will oscillate in the same time.*

For representing by AB [Fig. 27] the section of the pendulum by a plane which passes through C its centre of gravity, and supposing the points O′ and $O_,$ to be made the centres of suspension alternately, we have for l and l', the lengths of the corresponding simple pendulum,

$$l = a + \frac{k^2}{a} \text{ and } l' = a' + \frac{k^2}{a'},$$

a and a' denoting the distances O′C and $O_,C$ respectively. But if the oscillations of the two pendulums are made in the same time, we shall have

$$a + \frac{k^2}{a} = a' + \frac{k^2}{a'};$$

from which we get for a' the values a and $\frac{k^2}{a}$. But

$O'O_{,}$ the distance between the axes is equal to the sum of a and a'; hence we have

$$O'O_{,} = a + a';$$

or, employing the latter value of a',

$$O'O_{,} = a + \frac{k^2}{a}.$$

Hence $O'O_{,}$ is equal to the length of the simple pendulum which oscillates in the same time as the compound pendulum.

OF THE COLLISION OF BODIES.

52. We learn from experiment, 1°, that all bodies in nature are more or less compressible; and, 2°, that when in any case a body suffers compression, it tends in a greater or less degree to resume its primitive figure. The tendency of a body, when compressed, to resume its primitive figure, is called its *elasticity*. The elasticity of a body varies with the nature of its substance. The limiting cases of the elasticity of bodies are, 1st, the case in which the body tends to resume exactly its primitive figure; and, 2d, that in which it has no tendency in any degree to recover its figure. In the first case the body is said to be *perfectly elastic;* in the second, to be *inelastic*. Neither of these cases is found in nature: no known substance being either perfectly elastic, or entirely destitute of elasticity. All known sub-

stances are hence said to be *imperfectly elastic.* There are, however, some substances in which the elasticity approaches very near to the extreme cases.

53. *Inelastic bodies.*

Let A and B [Fig. 28], be two inelastic homogeneous bodies of spherical form, moving from left to right on the straight line A′B′ which joins the centres C and C′; and let A be supposed to have the greater velocity. When A overtakes B, a mutual compression will commence, which will continue for a very short time, till the bodies have acquired a common velocity. The two bodies will then cease to act upon each other, and will move with the common velocity as one body.

Let the masses of A and B be denoted by m and m', and their velocities before meeting by v and v' respectively, and let the common velocity which they have after meeting be denoted by u: then the velocity lost by A will be $v-u$, and the velocity gained by B will be $u-v'$, and the quantities of motion lost and gained will be $m(v-u)$ and $m'(u-v')$ respectively. Consequently, since by the third law of motion the force or quantity of motion lost by A must be equal to that gained by B, we shall have

$$m(v-u) = m'(u-v');$$

and hence

$$u = \frac{mv + m'v'}{m + m'}. \qquad \text{[a]}$$

The equation for the case in which the two bodies

move in opposite directions, may be immediately deduced from equation [a] by making v' negative. We shall thus have, for this case,

$$u = \frac{mv - m'v'}{m + m'}. \quad \text{[b]}$$

54. *Application of equations* [a] *and* [b] *to particular cases.*

1° Let one of the bodies, as B, be supposed at rest: then $v' = 0$, and we shall have

$$u = \frac{mv}{m + m'}.$$

In this case, we perceive that as m' increases, v and m being supposed to remain the same, u diminishes; and that when m' is so great that it may be considered infinite with respect to m, u is zero.

2° Let the bodies be supposed equal in mass; then $m = m'$; and accordingly as they move in the same or in opposite directions, we shall have

$$u = \tfrac{1}{2}(v + v'), \text{ or } \qquad u = \tfrac{1}{2}(v - v').$$

3° Let the bodies be supposed to be equal in mass, and one of them, as B, to be at rest: then $m = m'$ and $v' = 0$, and we shall have

$$u = \tfrac{1}{2}v.$$

55. *Elastic bodies.*

When a perfectly elastic body of spherical form impinges at right angles upon a fixed plane, its velocity is gradually diminished, and, when the compression reaches its limit, is reduced to zero; but the instant the compression is completed, the body, in virtue of its elasticity, begins to resume its primitive figure, and, in the operation, acquires a velocity in the opposite direction, exactly equal to that which was lost. Let us apply this result to the collision of two perfectly elastic spherical bodies A and B [Fig. 29], supposed to be moving from left to right on the line joining their centres; and let the same notation be employed as in the preceding case, Art. 53. In estimating the effect of the collision, it is evident that until the elasticity begins to act, we may consider the bodies as inelastic. Consequently at the instant of greatest compression, the velocity u common to each body will be given by the equation

$$u = \frac{mv + m'v'}{m + m'}; \qquad \text{[c]}$$

and the velocities lost by A and gained by B during the compression, will be

$$v - u \quad \text{and} \quad u - v'.$$

But in the process of resuming its primitive figure, each body may obviously be regarded as acting upon a fixed plane, supposed to pass through the point of meeting of the two bodies, at right angles to the line on which they are moving. Hence during this process A will lose, and B will gain, the additional velocities

$$v - u \quad \text{and} \quad u - v'$$

respectively, and the total velocities lost and gained by the two bodies will be

$$2(v - u) \quad \text{and} \quad 2(u - v')$$

respectively. If then we denote the velocity of A after collision by $v_{\prime}$, and the velocity of B by $v_{\prime\prime}$, we shall have

$$v_{\prime} = v - 2(v - u),$$

or

$$v_{\prime} = 2u - v;$$

and

$$v_{\prime\prime} = v' + 2(u - v'),$$

or

$$v_{\prime\prime} = 2u - v';$$

and substituting in these equations the value of u given by equation [c], we shall get

$$v_{\prime} = \frac{2(mv + m'v')}{m + m'} - v,$$

and

$$v_{\prime\prime} = \frac{2(mv + m'v')}{m + m'} - v',$$

or, reducing,

$$v_{\prime} = \frac{v(m - m') + 2m'v'}{m + m'}, \qquad \text{[d]}$$

and

$$v_{\prime\prime} = \frac{v'(m' - m) + 2mv}{m + m'}. \qquad \text{[e]}$$

To adapt these equations to the case in which the bodies move in opposite directions, we have only to suppose the velocity v' negative. We shall thus get

$$v_{\prime} = \frac{v(m - m') - 2m'v'}{m + m'}; \qquad \text{[f]}$$

$$v_{\prime\prime} = \frac{v'(m - m') + 2mv}{m + m'}. \qquad \text{[g]}$$

56. *Application of equations* [d] *and* [e].

1° Let $m = m'$: then

$$v_{\prime} = v', \quad \text{and} \quad v_{\prime\prime} = v.$$

Thus when the masses are equal, the collision will cause the bodies to exchange velocities.

2° Let $m = m'$ and $v' = 0$: then

$$v_{,} = 0, \quad \text{and} \quad v_{,,} = v.$$

That is, the body A will be brought to rest, and B will acquire its entire velocity; a result immediately deducible from the preceding case.

From this it is evident, that in the case of a series of elastic balls, A, B, C,...... P, Q, R, of equal mass, in contact with each other, and having their centres on the same straight line: if the first ball (A) be made to impinge with any velocity directly upon the second (B), the only visible effect will be to cause the last of the series (R) to move in the same direction with an equal velocity, all the intermediate balls remaining at rest.

3° When $v' = 0$, but m is not equal to m' the direction of the motion of the impinging ball, after collision, depends upon the relative values of m and m'. Thus when $m > m'$, $v_{,}$ and $v_{,,}$ are both positive, and both balls will move after collision in the original direction; but when $m < m'$, $v_{,,}$ is positive, but $v_{,}$ negative; and the impinged ball only will move in the original direction, while the impinging ball will rebound.

57. *Application of equations* [f] *and* [g].

1° Let $m = m'$: then

$$v_{,} = -v', \quad \text{and} \quad v_{,,} = v.$$

Thus, in this case, the bodies will exchange both velocities and directions.

2° Let $v = v'$: then

$$v_{,} = \frac{v(m - 3m')}{m + m'}, \text{ and } v_{,,} = \frac{v(3m - m')}{m + m'};$$

and we perceive that when $m = 3m'$, we have

$$v_{,} = 0, \quad \text{and} \quad v_{,,} = 2v.$$

58. *Relative velocity before and after collision.*

From the equations $v_{,} = 2u - v$, and $v_{,,} = 2u - v'$, we get by subtraction

$$v_{,} - v_{,,} = -(v - v');$$

from which it appears that the relative velocities of the two bodies before and after collision are equal to each other.

59. *Imperfectly elastic bodies.*

In the collision of an imperfectly elastic ball with a fixed plane, the ratio of the force or quantity of motion destroyed by the compression of the ball (or *the force of compression*), to the force generated by its restoration to its primitive figure (or *the force of restitution*), is called *the modulus of elasticity* of the substance of the ball. If, then, in any case, we denote the modulus by e, the mass of the ball by m, and the velocities corresponding to the forces of compression and restitution by c and r respectively, we shall have

$$e = \frac{mr}{mc} = \frac{r}{c};$$

and hence $r = ec.$ .... [h]

The value of e will obviously always lie between zero

and unity; the former limit answering to the case of an inelastic body, the latter to that of a body perfectly elastic.

To determine the velocities after collision, in the case of two imperfectly elastic balls moving on the line joining their centres, we proceed in the same manner as in Art. 55. Thus, employing the same notation as in that article, the velocities lost by A and gained by B during the compression, being

$$v - u \quad \text{and} \quad u - v',$$

the velocities lost and gained by the balls in the process of recovering their figure, will be [equa. h],

$$e(v - u) \quad \text{and} \quad e(u - v'),$$

and the total velocities lost and gained will be

$$(v - u) + e(v - u) \quad \text{and} \quad (u - v') + e(u - v').$$

Hence we shall have

$$\begin{aligned} v_{,} &= v - (v - u) - e(v - u) \\ &= (1 + e)\, u - ev \\ &= 1\,(+ e)\frac{mv + m'v'}{m + m'} - ev, \quad \ldots\ldots\ldots\ldots \text{[i]} \end{aligned}$$

and

$$\begin{aligned} v_{,,} &= v' + (u - v') + e\,(u - v') \\ &= (1 + e)\, u - ev' \\ &= (1 + e)\,\frac{mv + m'v'}{m + m'} - ev'. \quad \ldots\ldots\ldots\ldots \text{[k]} \end{aligned}$$

If we suppose the balls to have equal masses, and A to impinge upon B at rest, we have

$$m = m' \quad \text{and} \quad v' = 0;$$

and hence

$$v_{,,} = (1 + e)\,\frac{v}{2};$$

from which we get

$$e = \frac{2v_{//}}{v} - 1 \ldots\ldots\ldots\ldots\ldots\ldots \text{[m]}$$

To determine in a given case the modulus of elasticity, we suspend at the points C and C′ in the manner represented in Fig. 30, two equal spherical balls A and B of the substance in question; and withdrawing the one (A) from its position of equilibrium, suffer it to descend and impinge upon the other (B) at rest. The arcs described by the respective balls being MNG, M′N′G′, the velocities v and $v_{//}$ with which A impinges upon B, and which B acquires from the impulse, will be given [Art. 17] by the equations

$$v^2 = 2g \times \text{PG} = 2g \times \frac{\text{MG}^2}{\text{FG}},$$

$$v_{//}^2 = 2g \times \text{P'G'} = 2g \times \frac{\text{M'G'}^2}{\text{F'G'}}.$$

Hence, since FG = F′G′, we have

$$\frac{v_{//}}{v} = \sqrt{\frac{\text{P'G'}}{\text{PG}}} = \frac{\text{M'G'}}{\text{MG}};$$

and substituting this value of $\frac{v_{//}}{v}$ in equation [m], we get

$$e = 2\sqrt{\frac{\text{P'G'}}{\text{PG}}} - 1$$

$$= 2 \times \frac{\text{M'G'}}{\text{MG}} - 1.$$

The arcs MNG, M′N′G′ being known, their versed sines PG, P′G′, or their chords MG, M′G′, can be

K

easily calculated, and hence the value of e determined.

60. *Loss of living force in the collision of inelastic bodies.* The product of the mass of a material point (or of a body, all the points of which have the same velocity), by the square of its velocity, is called the *living force,* or *vis viva,* of the point or body.

Thus, employing the same notation as in article 53, the sum of the living forces of the inelastic spheres A and B, moving in the manner supposed in that article, is, before collision, $mv^2 + m'v'^2$; and after collision, $(m + m')u^2$. Let the latter of these expressions be subtracted from the former, and let their difference be denoted by d; then we shall have

$$d = mv^2 + m'v'^2 - (m + m')u^2.$$

But multiplying equation [a], (Art. 53,) by $(m + m')u$, we have

$$(m + m')u^2 = muv + m'uv',$$

and hence

$$0 = muv + m'uv' - (m + m')u^2; \ldots\ldots [\text{n}]$$

and adding these two equations, we get

$$(m + m')u^2 = 2muv + 2m'uv' - (m + m')u^2.$$

Consequently we have

$$d = mv^2 + m'v'^2 - 2muv - 2m'uv' + mu^2 + m'u^2$$

$$= m(v - u)^2 + m'(u - v')^2.$$

The second member of this equation being positive, it follows that in the case of the two inelastic spheres A and B, the sum of the living forces after collision is less than their sum before collision. It is also evident from the form of the second member, that the difference of the two sums, or the loss of living force by the collision, is equal to the sum of the living forces due to the velocities $(v - u)$ and $(u - v')$ which are lost and gained by the bodies respectively. This is a particular case of the general principle, that the sudden changes of velocity which occur in the collision of inelastic bodies, whatever their number and forms, and whether the collision takes place among themselves or with fixed obstacles, *are always attended with a loss of living force.*

61. *Conservation of living force in the collision of perfectly elastic bodies.*

If, as in article 55, we suppose the two spheres A and B to be perfectly elastic, employing the same notation as in that article, we shall have

$$v_{,} = 2u - v \quad \text{and} \quad v_{,,} = 2u - v';$$

and hence

$$mv_{,}^2 = m(2u - v)^2 \quad \text{and} \quad mv_{,,}^2 = m'(2u - v')^2.$$

Consequently we shall have

$$mv_{,}^2 + mv_{,,}^2 = m(4u^2 - 4uv + v^2) + m'(4u^2 - 4uv' + v'^2)$$
$$= 4(mu^2 + m'u^2 - muv - m'uv') + mv^2 + m'v'^2;$$

and since [Equa. n] the expression within the parenthesis is equal to zero, we shall get

$$mv_{,}^2 + mv_{,,}^2 = mv^2 + m'v'^2.$$

Thus in the case of the two perfectly elastic spheres A and B, the sum of the living forces before and after collision is the same. This is a particular case of the general principle, that *in the collision of perfectly elastic bodies, there is no loss of living force.*

62. *Conservation of the motion of the centre of gravity in the collision of bodies.*

Let the distances of the centres of the two spheres A and B from any assumed point of the line on which they are moving, at any instant before collision, be denoted by x and y; and let the distance of their common centre of gravity from the same point, at the same instant, be denoted by z: then, retaining the previous notation, we shall have (Art. 45. Statics)

$$(m + m')z = mx + my.$$

Again, let the corresponding distances from the same point, for the instant immediately following, be denoted by x', y' and z': we shall also have

$$(m + m')z' = mx' + my'.$$

Hence, subtracting the first equation from the second, we shall have

$$(m + m')(z' - z) = m(x' - x) + m'(y' - y);$$

and denoting the infinitely small interval between the two instants by t', and dividing each member of this equation by it, we shall get

$$(m + m')\frac{(z' - z)}{t'} = m\left(\frac{x' - x}{t'}\right) + m'\left(\frac{y' - y}{t'}\right).$$

If we suppose the second instant to be that which immediately precedes the collision, $\frac{x' - x}{t'}$ and $\frac{y' - y}{t'}$ will respectively express the velocities which we have denoted by v and v': Also $\frac{z'-z}{t'}$ will express the velocity, which we will denote by V, of the common centre of gravity of the two bodies. Hence we shall have

$$(m + m')\ V = mv + m'v',$$

and $$V = \frac{mv + m'v'}{m + m'} \ldots\ldots\ldots\ldots [o]$$

If we denote the velocities of A and B immediately after collision, by w and w', and the velocity of their common centre of gravity at the same instant by V', we shall find, by an operation similar to the above

$$V' = \frac{mw + m'w'}{m + m'}.$$

We will apply these results to the two extreme cases.

1° When the two bodies are inelastic, they have, after collision, the common velocity u. Hence, for this case, we have

$$w = w' = u,$$

and $$V' = \frac{(m + m')u}{m + m'} = u.$$

But [Art. 53] $$u = \frac{mv + m'v'}{m + m'};$$

hence [Equa. o] $$V = u,$$

and consequently $$V = V'.$$

2° When the bodies are perfectly elastic, we have

$$w = v_{,} = 2u - v, \quad \text{and} \quad w' = v_{,,} = 2u - v';$$

and hence

$$V' = \frac{m(2u - v) + m'(2u - v')}{m + m'}$$

$$= 2u - \frac{mv + m'v'}{m + m'}$$

$$= 2u - u = u.$$

But $V = u;$

consequently $V = V'.$

Thus whether the two bodies are inelastic or perfectly elastic, the velocity of their common centre of gravity, immediately before and after their meeting, is the same; the collision, though changing the velocity of each body, producing no alteration in the velocity of that point. This is a particular case of the general principle called "the principle of the conservation of the motion of the centre of gravity," that *the mutual action of the bodies of any system does not alter the motion of the centre of gravity of the system.*

63. *Oblique collision.*

We shall consider only the simple case of the collision of a spherical ball with an immovable plane. Let AB [Fig. 31] represent the plane, and CI the line described by the centre of the ball. On CI produced, let IE be taken to represent the velocity of the ball; and let it be resolved into the components IF and IM, the one in the plane AB, the other perpendicular to it. Denoting the velocity of the ball by v, and CIL the *angle of incidence* by a, we shall have

$$\text{IF} = v \sin a, \quad \text{and} \quad \text{IM} = v \cos a.$$

1° If the ball is inelastic, there will be no component perpendicular to the plane after collision, and the ball will move in the plane with the velocity $v \sin a$.

2° If the ball is perfectly elastic, it will tend to rebound in the direction IL with the velocity IN, equal to IM or $v \cos a$; and in virtue of the two velocities IF and IN, will move in the direction IG with a velocity ID, equal to IE; the *angle of reflection* GIL being equal to the angle of incidence.

3° If the ball is imperfectly elastic, it will tend to rebound with a velocity IN′ less than IN, and such, that if e denote the modulus of elasticity, we shall have

$$e = \frac{\text{IN}'}{\text{IN}},$$

and hence $$\text{IN}' = e \times \text{IN}.$$

In this case the ball will move, after collision, in the direction IG′, and with a velocity ID′ which will be given by the equation

$$\text{ID}' = \sqrt{v^2 \sin^2 a + e^2 v^2 \cos^2 a};$$

and if we denote the angle of reflection LIG′ by a', this angle will be given by the equation

$$\text{tang } a' = \frac{v \sin a}{ev \cos a} = \frac{\text{tang a}}{e}.$$

GRAVITATION.

64. It has been found by observation, that the planets, in their revolutions about the sun, observe the following laws:

1st. The areas described by the radius vector of a planet (or the line drawn from the centre of the sun to the centre of the planet), are as the times employed in describing them.

2d. The orbit of a planet is an ellipse of small eccentricity, having the centre of the sun at one of its foci.

3d. The squares of the periodic times of any two planets (or the times of the complete revolution of each about the sun), are to each other as the cubes of their mean distances from the sun (or the semi-transverse axes of their orbits).

The satellites, in their revolutions about their primaries, are found to obey the same laws.

These laws, from the name of their discoverer, are called *Kepler's laws.*

According to the first law of motion, the tendency of a planet, at each point of its orbit, is to move in the straight line which is tangent to its orbit at that point: therefore, since its motion is curvilinear, it must constantly be acted upon by an accelerating force. The object of this section is very briefly to investigate the laws which regulate this force. The laws of Kepler refer to the motions of the centres of gravity of the planets; and in all that follows, we shall consider the masses of the planets as reduced to these points.

1° *The direction of the force.*

Since the areas described by the radius vector of a planet are proportional to the times employed in describing them, the force which deflects the planet from the straight line in which it tends to move, must (Art. 22), coincide in direction with the radius vector, and *constantly solicit the body towards the centre of the sun.*

2° *Law according to which the intensity of the force varies.*

Let AMA′ [Fig. 32] represent the elliptical orbit of a planet, and F the focus occupied by the centre of the sun. Let MM″ be an arc described by the planet in the indefinitely short time t'; and to its extremities M and M″, draw the radii vectores FM and FM″. Draw MY tangent to the curve at M; and from M and F, draw MC′ and FY perpendicular to MY. Draw also M″N, M″K perpendicular to MC′ and MF respectively; and take MC′ equal to the radius of curvature at the point M.

The arc MM″ being infinitely small, the direction and intensity of the accelerating force, during the time t', may be supposed to remain the same. During this time, then, the accelerating force acting alone would cause the point to describe the line MI. Hence denoting the intensity of the force by F, we have [Art 3],

$$\text{MI} = \tfrac{1}{2}Ft'^2;$$

and taking t' for the unit of time, we get

$$F = 2\text{MI}. \qquad \text{[a]}$$

To find an expression for MI, we get from the similar triangles MNI, M″KI,

$$\text{M}''\text{K} : \text{M}''\text{I} :: \text{MN} : \text{MI};$$

and hence $$\text{MI} = \text{MN} \times \frac{\text{M}''\text{I}}{\text{M}''\text{K}}. \qquad \text{[b]}$$

But since MM″ may be considered the arc of a circle of which MC′ is the radius, we have

$$\text{M}''\text{N}^2 = (2\text{MC}' - \text{MN})\text{MN};$$

or, neglecting MN in comparison with 2MC′,

$$\text{M}''\text{N}^2 = 2\text{MC}' \times \text{MN};$$

and hence $$\text{MN} = \frac{\text{M}''\text{N}^2}{2\text{MC}'}$$

$$= \frac{\text{M}''\text{I}^2}{2\text{MC}'}.^* \qquad \text{[c]}$$

Moreover, we have

$$\text{MC}' = \frac{p}{2} \times \left(\frac{\text{FM}}{\text{FY}}\right)^3, \dagger$$

(p denoting the parameter of the ellipse); or, observing that the similar triangles M″KI, FYM give

$$\text{FM} : \text{FY} :: \text{M}''\text{I} : \text{M}''\text{K},$$

or $$\frac{\text{FM}}{\text{FY}} = \frac{\text{M}''\text{I}}{\text{M}''\text{K}},$$

we have $$\text{MC}' = \frac{p}{2} \times \left(\frac{\text{M}''\text{I}}{\text{M}''\text{K}}\right)^3:$$

* NI may be neglected in comparison with M″I, since it is a quantity of the same order as MN; that is, an infinitely small quantity of the second order.

† Jackson's Conic Sections, Chap. VI, Prop. I, Cor. 2.

hence substituting this value of the radius vector in equation [c], we get

$$MN = \frac{1}{p} \times \frac{M''K^3}{M''I} \text{ .... [d]}$$

Lastly, substituting this value of MN in equation [b], we have

$$MI = \frac{1}{p} \times M''K^2 \text{. .... [e]}$$

If now we denote the area of the elliptical sector FMM″ by s, we have (considering MM″ as a straight line),

$$s = \frac{FM \times M''K}{2},$$

and hence $$M''K^2 = \frac{4s^2}{FM^2};$$

and substituting this value of $M''K^2$ in equation [e], we get

$$MI = \frac{1}{p} \times \frac{4s^2}{FM^2}:$$

hence [Equa. a] we have

$$F = \frac{2}{p} \times \frac{4s^2}{FM^2} \text{. .... [f]}$$

Again, considering the action of the accelerating force at some other point of the ellipse, as M′, and for an equal interval of time (t'), we have, denoting the intensity of the force by F',

$$F' = \frac{2}{p} \times \frac{4s^2}{FM'^2}:$$

consequently we have

$$F : F' :: \text{FM}'^2 : \text{FM}^2.$$

Thus the force which retains the planet in its orbit, *varies in the inverse ratio of the square of the distance of the planet from the centre of the sun.*

65. *Variations of the force from one planet to another.*

Let T and T' denote the periodic times of two planets; s and s', the areas described by their radii vectores in the time t'; and a and b, a' and b', the semi-axes of their orbits: then the area described by the radius vector of the first planet, in the time T, will be Ts; but this area, being the entire surface of the ellipse, will also be expressed by πab; hence we shall have

$$Ts = \pi ab,$$

and

$$T = \frac{\pi ab}{s}.$$

We shall also have

$$T' = \frac{\pi a'b'}{s'}:$$

consequently, according to Kepler's third law, we shall have

$$\frac{\pi^2 a^2 b^2}{s^2} : \frac{\pi^2 a'^2 b'^2}{s'^2} :: a^3 : a'^3;$$

or, multiplying the antecedents by $\frac{s^2}{a^3}$ and the consequents by $\frac{s'^2}{a'^3}$,

$$\frac{b^2}{a} : \frac{b'^2}{a'} :: s^2 : s'^2;$$

or, denoting the parameters of the ellipses by p and p',

$$s^2 \ : \ s'^2 \ :: \ \frac{p}{2} \ : \ \frac{p'}{2}.$$

But denoting the accelerating forces which act upon the two planets at the points **M** and **M**, of their orbits, by F and $F_{,}$, we have (Equa. f, Art. 64)

$$F \ : \ F_{,} \ :: \ \frac{1}{p} \times \frac{s^2}{\text{FM}^2} \ : \ \frac{1}{p'} \times \frac{s'^2}{\text{FM}_{,}^2}.$$

Combining then this proportion with that immediately preceding, we get

$$F \ : \ F_{,} \ :: \ \text{FM}_{,}^2 \ : \ \text{FM}^2.$$

From this we infer that the force which solicits the planets towards the centre of the sun, varies from one planet to another according to the same law as that which governs in different positions of the same planet; the variation depending only upon the distance, and not upon any peculiarities that may exist in the constitution of the planets themselves.

66. Since the satellites, in their revolutions about their primaries, also conform to Kepler's laws, the force which retains them in their orbits must solicit them towards the centres of their primaries, according to the same law as that which obtains in the case of the sun and planets.

67. From the foregoing results, it is inferred that the matter of the bodies composing the solar system is endowed with a peculiar property, in virtue of which these bodies exert a mutual attraction according to the above law.

With respect to the relation between the attraction exerted by a body, and the mass of the body, the most obvious supposition, viz. that the force is directly proportional to the mass, is found to agree with the results of observation and calculation.

Lastly, it can be shown, by methods not adapted to the present work, that if bodies, considered in the aggregate, attract each other in the inverse ratio of the squares of their mutual distances, then their ultimate particles must attract each other according to the same law. We thus arrive at the general law, *that the particles of all bodies attract each other in the direct ratio of their masses, and the inverse ratio of the squares of their distances.* This law is called *the law or theory of universal gravitation.* Its full development in its application to the bodies of the solar system, constitutes the science of *physical astronomy.* The agreement of the deductions of this science with the results of observation, is such as perfectly to establish the truth of the law.

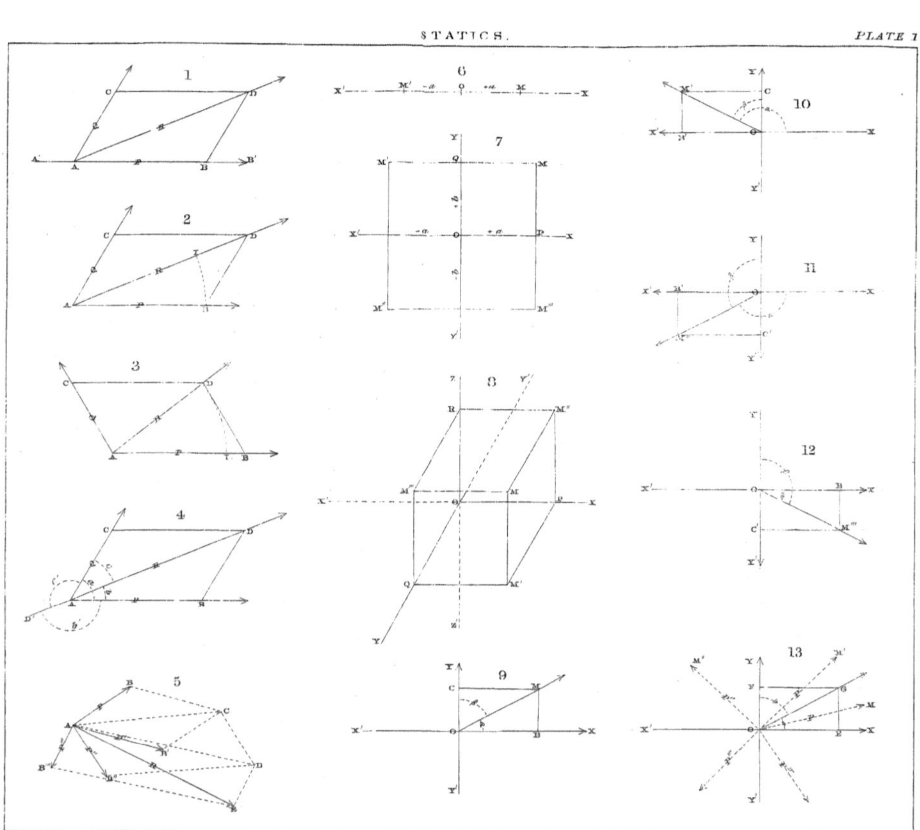

Engraved & Printed by J. E. Gavit, Albany.

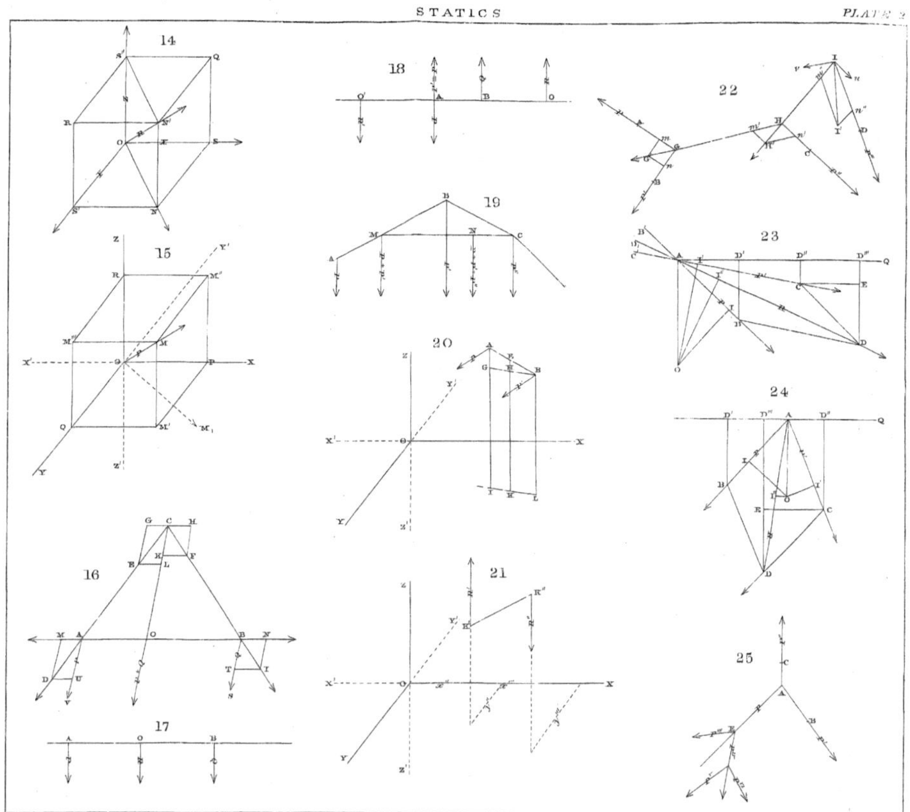

Engraved & Printed by J. E. Gavit, Albany.

Engraved & Printed by J.E.Gavit,Albany.

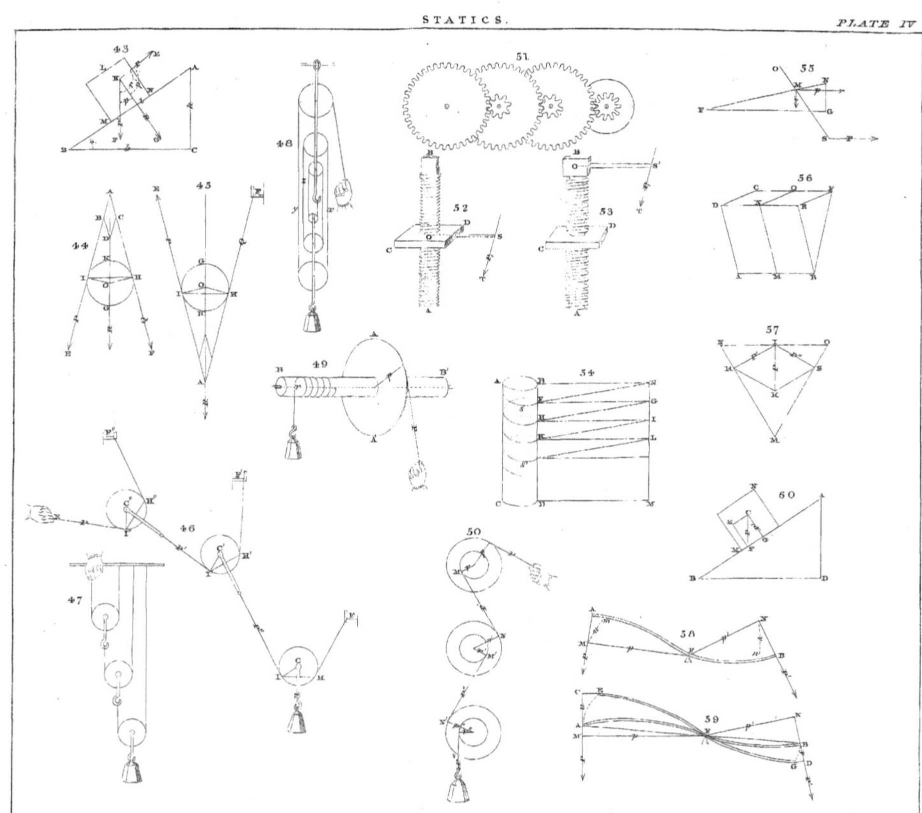

Engraved & Printed by J.E. Gavit, Albany

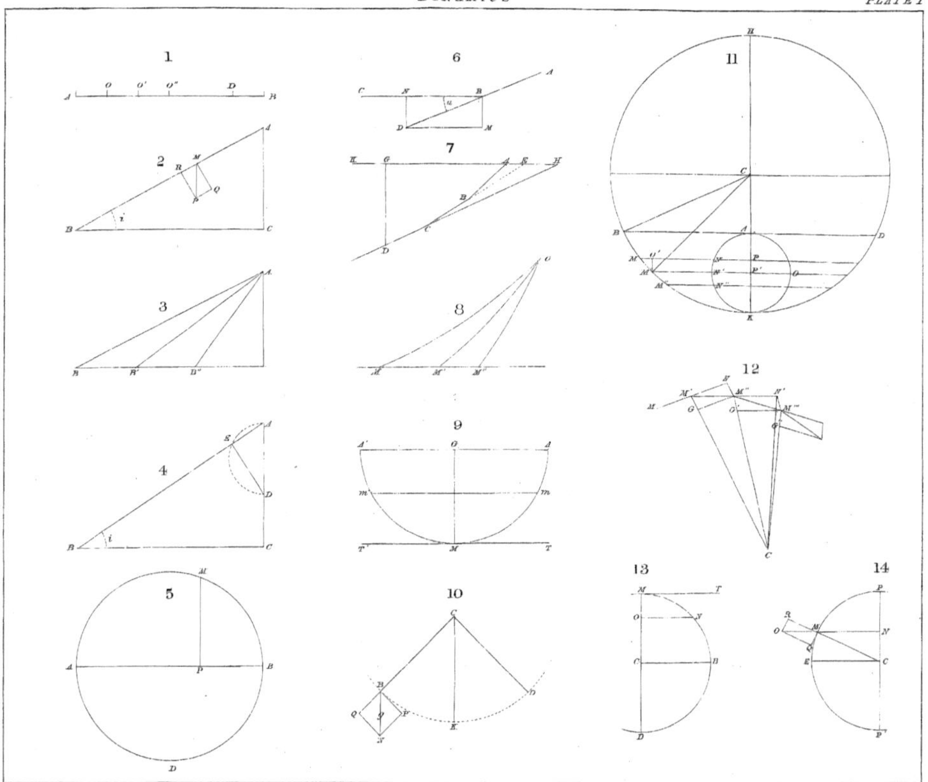

Engraved & Printed by [illegible]

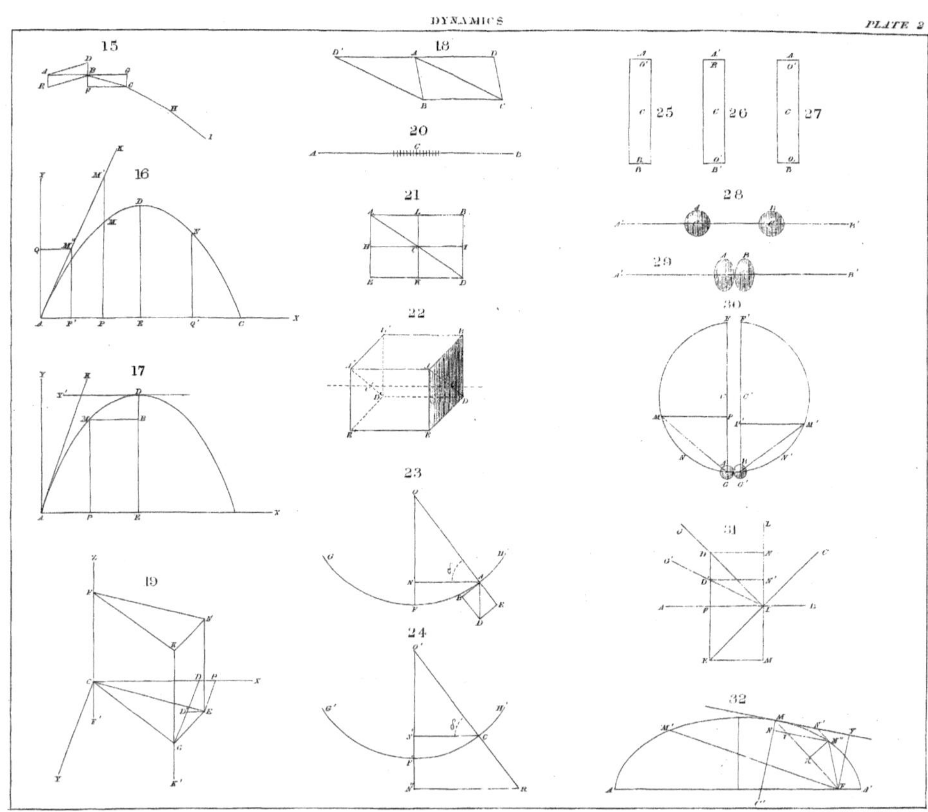
15
16
17
18
19
20
21
22
23
24
25
26
27
28
29
30
31
32